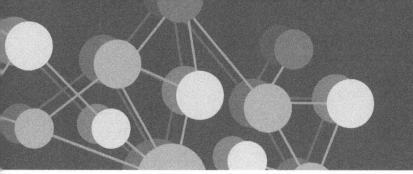

WIRED TO CONNECT

The Brain Science of Teams and a New Model
for Creating Collaboration and Inclusion

Britt Andreatta, PhD

7th Mind
Publishing

D1041747

**7th Mind
Publishing**

This edition March 2018.
7th Mind Publishing
Santa Barbara, California

The Four Gates to Peak Team Performance™ and Change Quest™ are registered trademarks of 7th Mind, Inc.

To book Dr. Andreatta for speaking engagements please contact Jacqui Sneathen at Speaking@BrittAndreatta.com, or visit www.BrittAndreatta.com/speaking.

For learning and training solutions based on this book, please visit www.7thMindInc.com.

For order or bulk purchases of this book, please write Orders@7thMindPublishing.com.

Printing by Dog Ear Publishing
www.dogearpublishing.net

ISBN: 978-0-9973547-5-1 (paper)
ISBN: 978-0-9973547-4-4 (ebook)

This book is printed on acid-free paper.
Printed in the United States of America.

To the amazing Gate 4 teams I have been a part of
and the leaders who knew how to get us there.

CONTENTS

IV: The Brain Science of Inclusion & Trust

V: A New Model: The Four Gates to Peak Team Performance™

VI: Strategies for Executives, Team Leaders, & Team Members

INTRODUCTION: FINDING THE I IN TEAM

"There is no I in team."
Vernon Law, baseball player, 1960

Most of us have heard that phrase at some point in our lives. I certainly have—in fact, that quote has sat on my desk in every place I have ever worked. But you know what? It's wrong.

When I started researching the neuroscience of teams, I wasn't aware that I would end up questioning such an iconic belief. But the brain science of what brings out the best in groups points us in a new and surprising direction.

The best teams, the highest-performing ones, create a cohesive unit *through* honoring each member's unique contributions and making them feel included and valued for who they are, as individuals.

It turns out there is an I in team. In fact there are lots of I's. Every team is made up of individuals who bring their own perspectives, skill sets, and experiences. Not only do team environments need to leverage the gifts of those individuals, the group needs to make its members feel safe enough to bring their best work forward. When this is done right, members feel they belong and the group is set up to achieve a rarified state of peak performance, one that is neurologically different from the rest.

Today, teams power the majority of work done in organizations around the world. And every day, they are expected to navigate between coordination, cooperation, and collaboration, each representing different levels of complexity and requiring different skills. But true collaboration requires special conditions, ones that are much more difficult to create than you might think.

My intention for this book is to offer clear steps on how to create those conditions. I know from my consulting work with all kinds of organizations that collaboration is where the real juicy stuff lives. It's also the place of greatest struggle.

This is why teams are perhaps the single most important entity in today's workplace: When we get them right, we leverage so many powerful aspects of human biology that can propel both individuals and the organization forward. But getting it wrong can cripple an organization's ability to compete or succeed.

As with my previous books, *Wired to Connect* was born out of my own experience. As a consultant, I help organizations of all kinds work through a variety of challenges, and team performance certainly tops the list. And of course, I have been a team member and team leader many times throughout my career. Those experiences are the source of some of my greatest professional joys and the most difficult challenges. Now I know why and I am eager to share this knowledge with you.

This book is organized into six sections:

I.   We'll begin by understanding what teams look like in today's organizations along with the difference between collaboration, coordination and cooperation.

II.   Next, we'll dive into the brain science of groups and teams, particularly what sets them up for "good" performance.

III.   We'll also explore the brain science of safety and belonging, two critical factors in the early development of any team.

IV.   Next, we'll examine why inclusion and trust are pivotal for reaching optimal performance.

V.   Then I will introduce you to my new Four Gates to Peak Team Performance™ model that synthesizes all of the research into an effective tool you can use in any setting.

VI.   We'll end with specific tips and strategies for building successful teams, whether you're a member or its leader.

My Research Process

I have been studying the science of success for over 20 years. All thoughts, beliefs, and behaviors start in the brain and neuroscience offers unique and valuable insights into how we can bring out the best in people and organizations. In my research, I always source validated studies. As someone who completed a PhD at one of the world's top-ranked research universities, I know that rigorous research practices are designed to keep us from being mislead or manipulated. The ethical standards for academic research are incredibly high, to protect against the forces of favoritism, politics, and popularity. That is why I look to experienced scientists and research centers that follow the right protocols to ensure their studies are reliable and valid.

I also explore a topic across a wide spectrum of disciplines from neuroscience to psychology and biology to organizational development. This broad view allows me to create models and solutions that are validated from many perspectives and represent the best that the brightest minds have to offer. All of my sources are listed in the References section at the end of the book.

Case Studies

Throughout the book, you will find fourteen case studies illustrating teams that are either succeeding or struggling. While I love geeking out on scientific studies, it's important to apply those findings outside of the lab to our real, everyday workplace challenges. So, I put out a call for case studies about current teams to gather stories and look at what's working when they go well and what's missing when they go poorly. It allowed me to compare what scientists are seeing in their labs with actual working teams. I received over 50 submissions from all kinds of organizations: small businesses, corporations (including Fortune 500), educational institutions, government agencies, and nonprofits. Submissions came from every industry including health care, technology, finance, manufacturing, media, and retail.

These case studies are shared with permission and written by the submitters, who were either team members or the team's leader. The only editing I did was to fix the occasional typo. Each one brings to life key concepts from the book but, more importantly, I think they demonstrate how common these experiences are. Nearly all of them resonated with me personally because they so closely matched my own experiences with teams.

You'll find the case studies set apart in boxes with the organization type and size listed. Small organizations have up to 500 employees; medium organizations have 501 to 5,000 employees, and large have more than 5,000 employees. Many organizations are global, operating in regions around the world.

This book is written for working people everywhere. Whether you are a team member or the team leader, you'll find useful tips and strategies you can implement today. In addition, I used this research to build new team training programs for leaders, managers, and employees. If you want to learn more, visit www.7thMindInc.com.

Let's get started!

Take a Learning Journey

I have learned that before I can write a book, I have to teach the concepts and content to live audiences. I always try to create a learning experience that shifts people's knowledge and behaviors. Before I wrote this book, I taught this content through workshops and presentations at conferences and corporations. In a live presentation, I model best practices in learning design based on the research of my previous book, *Wired to Grow: Harness the Power of Brain Science to Master Any Skill*. This includes having the audience pause and reflect on content every so often, applying it to their current situation.

Engaging with concepts in a personal way helps the brain learn and retain material and, more importantly, it's where any meaningful shift in actions starts. To help you gain the most from this book, you will find this light bulb icon marking an element called "Your Learning Journey" at the end of each section. Each includes instructions for applying the content to your experiences. I recommend that you use these sections to build your confidence and competence with skills that create team success.

To make this easier, I have created a free downloadable PDF for you to fill out as you explore each concept (www.BrittAndreatta.com/ Wired-to-Connect). To maximize your experience, I also recommend you find a partner to share with. Social learning actually boosts long-term retention, and when you work in partnership you both gain the insights of each other's experiences. So ask a friend or colleague who works in a team environment and explore the content together.

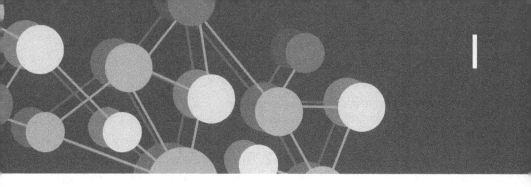

THE POWER OF TEAMS TODAY

"Not finance. Not strategy. Not technology. It is teamwork that is the ultimate competitive advantage, both because it is so powerful and so rare."

Patrick Lencioni, *The Five Dysfunctions of a Team*

1. The Rise of Teams

Teams power more and more of today's work. In fact, according to research by Ken Blanchard Companies, nearly 90 percent of workers say that they spend one-third to one-half of each day working in teams. This reflects a shift in how organizations structure their functions and employees: Past organizations were built on hierarchical models, which were efficient at the time. In today's fast-moving world, that structure has proven ineffective as it creates silos and slows down communication and innovation.

Around the world and across every sector, more and more organizations are moving to team-based models, organizing employees into smaller groups that are more nimble and flexible. In their *The State of Teams* whitepaper, the Center for Creative Leadership (CCL) writes, "In the age of lean organizations, one could assert that most work groups in existence today are being pushed to evolve (formally and informally) toward a team philosophy as the span of control of management widens and pressures to outperform competition increase."

In their survey of executives from a wide range of industries, CCL discovered that 91 percent believe that teams are central to organizational success. And 95 percent stated that people are participating on more than one team at a time. This new norm means that teams are not just self-sufficient units but actually networks, collaborating across organizational and geographical boundaries.

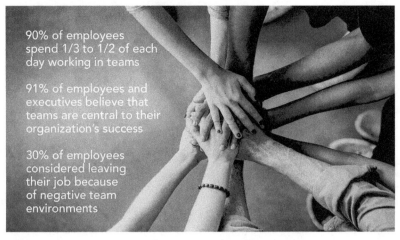

90% of employees spend 1/3 to 1/2 of each day working in teams

91% of employees and executives believe that teams are central to their organization's success

30% of employees considered leaving their job because of negative team environments

Data on teams in today's workplaces

According to research by Bersin and Associates, a global leader in talent-management issues, we have entered a new phase in the evolution of management thinking, which they call "networks of teams."

A study by Deloitte, a worldwide network of consulting services, found that "networks of teams" was a rising trend and a number-one ranked issue, with 92 percent of respondents stating that redesigning the organization was a top priority. According to the authors of the *2016 Global Human Capital Trends* report, "Companies are decentralizing authority, moving toward product- and customer-centric organizations, and forming dynamic networks of highly empowered teams that communicate and coordinate activities in unique and powerful ways."

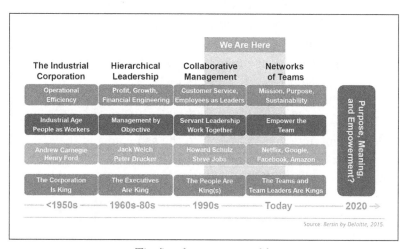

Timeline of management models
Used with permission from Deloitte Consulting, LLP

In the past, organizations used hierarchical leadership with a focus on management by objectives (MBOs) or key performance indicators (KPIs); then we segued to an era of collaborative management where employee engagement and customer service were top priorities. Now we are entering a new phase where the focus has shifted to networks of teams along with mission, purpose, and sustainability. The authors state, "These companies do away with the idea that you are a leader because of your position—and focus on people developing 'followership,' and building the systems and tools, which let people cross-communicate easily."

The study also revealed that less than one-quarter of large companies are organized functionally today. All of the world's largest employment countries list new organizational design as a top priority with China at 97 percent, India at 91 percent, United States at 91 percent and Canada at 89 percent.

Our images of teams are changing too. The word "team" often evokes sports teams (from your favorite professional sport to your local youth league) or knowledge workers sitting around a conference table. But in reality teams abound in every type of work environment and industry. Consider these common examples:

- Medical professionals in an operating room or clinic
- Engineers coding a cloud-based product
- Soldiers in a military unit on patrol
- Musicians in a band or orchestra
- Dancers of all types
- Firefighters putting down a blaze
- Personnel on an oil rig shift
- Line workers at a manufacturing plant
- Chefs and servers in a restaurant

Teams are also shifting in forms. A team used to be a group of people working together in person in the same area at the same time. Now it's just as likely to include people from another region, or even country, thanks to technology and web-based work tools.

2. Teams in Trouble

While we shift to this new way of working, organizations face new challenges as they expect people to work in previously unprecedented ways. As mentioned, many teams now comprise members from around the world. This can make coworking difficult as people navigate time and space, as well as cultural and linguistic differences, in order to communicate and collaborate. Often mediated through a computer screen or phone line, workers are expected to accomplish elaborate feats while never meeting face to face.

When I worked at LinkedIn, a company with 10,000-plus employees scattered around the globe, it was a common practice to build global teams. I worked regularly with people I had not met in person. While the company was headquartered in California, we would rotate meetings from early mornings to late evenings so that colleagues in Europe, the Middle East, and Asian Pacific regions could participate during their regular workdays.

Today, many organizations ask their employees and teams to align their work time to the normal business hours of their customers and clients whether it's across the country or the planet. This is the reality of doing global business—someone has to be available 24 hours per day, seven days per week, 365 days per year. For global teams, it means that the group is never really "off duty" or taking a break at the same time. While it might seem that this moves work forward faster, in my experience negotiating work projects around various national holidays can often slow projects down for weeks when a team needs input and buy-in from everyone involved.

In addition, building relationships is difficult because every meeting is scheduled and focused on the task at hand, so those "water cooler" conversations about a breaking news story or the latest episode of a favorite show just don't happen as easily. And when relationship-building is shortchanged, it's harder to build trust, which in turn may lead to more conflict, decreased productivity, and ultimately attrition. In fact, the *Organizational Team Dynamics Survey* found that 30 percent of employees considered leaving their job because of negative team environments. High turnover can be devastating because the group's development not only pauses but backtracks every time a team member leaves and is replaced.

Over time, this can create employee disengagement. It's estimated that disengaged employees cost organizations over $550 billion per year in the United States alone. In fact, Gallup's research has found that 16 percent of US workers are actively disengaged and that the real costs of a disengaged employee is equivalent to 34 percent of their salary. But what about the rest of the world? Gallup's *2017 State of the Global Workplace* report shows that 18 percent of global employees are actively disengaged, with country- and region-specific data. For example, if a 20,000-person company was half composed of US workers and half from other countries, that would mean approximately 3,400 employees are actively disengaged. If the average salary is $60,000, the annual cost is nearly $70 million!

Calculating the Cost of Actively Disengaged Employees		
	United States	Global
Headcount	10,000	10,000
Number of disengaged	1,600 (16%)	1,800 (18%)
Median salary	$60,000/year	
Cost of disengagement	34% of salary	
Cost per disengaged employee	$20,400/year	
Cost per year	$32,640,000	$36,720,000
TOTAL COST PER YEAR	$69,360,000/year	

Example of the costs of disengagement

While disengagement is expensive, that number does not account for the additional costs that mount when an employee leaves. The Society for Human Resource Management (SHRM) estimates that losing an employee can cost anywhere from 50 to 250 percent of their annual salary plus benefits. This includes the cost of recruiting and hiring, the lost productivity of the unfilled role, and the time it takes for the new hire to get up to speed and become fully productive.

The percentage range maps to position level. Entry-level positions cost 50 percent of their salary plus benefits to replace, while higher-level or skilled positions (for example, IT or engineering) are closer to 250 percent.

Disengagement and attrition only represent some of the potential costs. A team that fails to deliver on a project can cause enormous consequences, especially in today's fast-paced world where innovation and time-to-market can make or break a company.

Take for example the recent debacle at Equifax, where the cyber security team's failure to implement a security patch resulted in the hack of personal data for millions of people. The stock plummeted and federal officials launched an investigation.

While this seems to be a unique and dramatic case, "typical" team failures can still be enormously costly. *Harvard Business Review* analyzed over 1,400 IT projects and found, on average, schedule overruns ranged from 27 to 70 percent, and cost overruns by as much as 200 percent.

Gallup states, in their *Cost of Bad Project Management* business journal, "Cost and time overruns also have a profound effect on national economies. One estimate of IT failure rates is between 5 percent and 15 percent, which represents a loss of $50 billion to $150 billion per year in the United States. Another study estimated that IT project failures cost the European Union €142 billion."

Errors such as these have driven consumer trust to an all-time low. In fact, in the PricewaterhouseCoopers *21st Global CEO Survey*, 69 percent of CEOs say it's harder for businesses to sustain trust in the digital age because of all the issues surrounding cyber security and site reliability.

IT is not the only industry where team failures lead to big costs. Boston residents experienced enormous frustration when the Central Artery/Tunnel Project, known as "The Big Dig," took years longer than anticipated and cost taxpayers nearly double the original estimate. Similar challenges for residents and officials have been seen in Europe, with the Channel Tunnel.

And, of course, costs can be immeasurable. Like the loss of seven precious lives when the Columbia Shuttle burned up during reentry in 2003 or the hundreds of thousands of deaths each year attributed to medical error in hospitals and clinics around the world.

Case Study: System of Hospitals
Org Size: Large

"I am working to assist a senior leadership team in standardizing goals across five hospitals. They are a mix of five long-term

---

nursing leaders and five brand-new physician leaders. While our motto is team-based leadership, our hospital cultures are actually competitive. Each of these senior leaders has competing priorities being given to them from throughout our system. In addition, each of the hospitals is going through significant restructuring at high- and mid-leadership levels.

Our retreats are focused on communication standards, speaking on behalf of this team when around others, decision-making (process and authority), and agreeing to behavioral standards. The group needs to become more comfortable with challenging the status quo through asking open-ended questions. But the leader of this team is not connected to the needs of the group and little progress is being made with coaching. The leader needs to be providing feedback on behaviors and decisions but seems to have no awareness when the team is heading in the right or wrong direction.

This team is trying to create change with zero leader support and is challenged to form and manage itself in the midst of the chaos surrounding it."

So while we are moving to this new era of teams as an organizational structure, these examples show that we have not equipped today's professionals with the knowledge and skills to be effective team members or leaders…yet. Teams that tackle complex projects, or deal with high-stakes work, or who work in highly uncertain situations need special skills. And yet, most teams don't receive much, if any, special training on how to work effectively as a team, nor are they given the time and support needed to build the most effective relationships among the members.

My research into the brain science of teams has yielded a new understanding of how we bring out the best in groups, and a model that can be implemented in every type of organization.

3. Understanding Groups

Before we dive in to the brain structures that impact groups and teams, it's important to understand some elements of group development. For over 50 years, Dr. Bruce Tuckman's research has been the go-to source of understanding groups. His five-stage model of group development has stood the test of time because it unwittingly rests on the biology of how humans work together.

Tuckman studied all kinds of groups and found that they develop through five distinct stages. Here is how they play out in the workplace:

1. **Forming:** The group meets each other and learns about the focus of their work together. At this stage, formalities are preserved as people are sizing each other up and figuring out their role in the group and on the task.

2. **Storming:** Members start to communicate their views from their individual perspectives. As differences are discovered in their views or approaches to the task, conflict arises—a natural, normal, and even healthy element of this stage. Concerned team leaders must avoid pushing the group to false harmony or allowing toxic patterns to get established. We'll explore conflict more in coming chapters.

3. **Norming:** Moving through conflict ushers in this stage. Members start to feel part of the group. Cohesion is established when the group realizes that they can achieve their goals if they incorporate their various strengths. Each understands more clearly how they can make meaningful contributions to the goal.

4. **Performing:** The team, having created an open and trusting atmosphere, succeeds at tasks and grows together. This high-performance phase often ushers in a new round of healthy conflict as people share ideas for how to improve the product or process. Differences are welcomed as the group drives to achieve success. People are also less concerned with hierarchy and more interested in engaging with each other from a place of respect and trust.

5. **Adjourning or Mourning:** This stage is about completing the project and dispersing the team. Members wrap up their time together, making meaning of the experience by celebrating their successes, evaluating the project or process (for example, a summary report), and creating a transition plan for members as needed.

It's important to remember that Tuckman conducted his research in the 1960s and 70s when most research subjects were white men. Recently, scholars like University of Iowa's Dr. Jill Scott-Cawiezell, Dr. Maria Ward, and Kirstin Manges have noted that today's workplaces have fewer complete endings, and that this last stage may not be an ending but rather a reconfiguring, to expand projects and integrate new team members. Called "outperforming" or "transforming," this stage is almost a relaunch of the forming phase, as the group has to align to the new members and make shifts in the project or task.

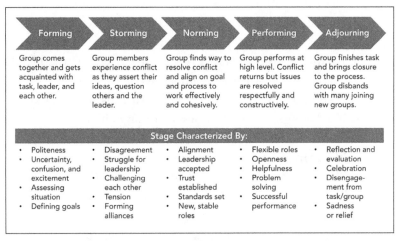

Forming	Storming	Norming	Performing	Adjourning
Group comes together and gets acquainted with task, leader, and each other.	Group members experience conflict as they assert their ideas, question others and the leader.	Group finds way to resolve conflict and align on goal and process to work effectively and cohesively.	Group performs at high level. Conflict returns but issues are resolved respectfully and constructively.	Group finishes task and brings closure to the process. Group disbands with many joining new groups.

Stage Characterized By:				
• Politeness • Uncertainty, confusion, and excitement • Assessing situation • Defining goals	• Disagreement • Struggle for leadership • Challenging each other • Tension • Forming alliances	• Alignment • Leadership accepted • Trust established • Standards set • New, stable roles	• Flexible roles • Openness • Helpfulness • Problem solving • Successful performance	• Reflection and evaluation • Celebration • Disengagement from task/group • Sadness or relief

Characteristics of Tuckman's stages

4. Tuckman Today

I have worked with and supervised teams for years and find Tuckman's model to be a great tool for understanding and supporting a group's development. These linear stages are easily observable for groups that start and end together, because each of the stages is clearly delineated. Here are some types of such groups:

- A team formed to complete a specific project
- Volunteers responding to a natural disaster
- A group hosting a major event, like a conference or concert
- Resident assistants at a college freshman residence hall
- A building crew for a new urban high-rise

Even established groups, which make up the majority of workplaces today, still go through a version of Tuckman's model. As various members leave and join, the group will backtrack as it reconfigures itself. For example, when a colleague leaves for a new job, the rest of the group has to figure out how to keep working effectively until a new person is brought in. And even when that new person arrives, it can take weeks or months for them to become a fully effective and integrated member of the team.

This again is why SHRM estimates that the cost of turnover is 50 to 250 percent of the employee's annual salary, plus benefits. It takes time for the new person to get up to speed and fully productive.

While continuous turnover wasn't as much of an issue in our parents' day, when people stayed at a company for decades, today's average job tenure is three and a half to four years; for organizations with high attrition it can be even shorter.

This means that most of today's teams are in a perpetual cycle of forming-storming-norming, rarely if ever getting to the performing stage. As a result, teams cannot easily get to effective collaboration or engage in true innovation. Needless to say, this can cost an organization millions of dollars in lost productivity, as well as attrition of their best people and the high costs of employee disengagement. This next case study illustrates this perfectly.

Case Study: Global Tech Company
Size: Large

"I work in HR at a global tech company. The VP of Product loves to reorganize the team, using it as his primary tool to solve every problem. It's common for people to have five or six managers a year. He doesn't fully understanding the negative impact of the constant shuffling. At first, the employees gave it their best effort. This is one of the top companies in the world, and the perks and salary are great. But over time, it's getting harder and harder for them, which is reflected in dropping engagement scores and higher turnover. As one employee said, 'I just never feel like I can do my best work here. I'm always trying to figure out a new boss, or get used to a new team, and just when we start to settle in, we are shifted again. I haven't been able to really dig in on a project for over a year.'

Another said, 'I know people think it's great to work here but if you really pay attention, there is a lot of turnover. All of the excited folks are new but over time, they learn what the rest of us did, which is not to care too much about your work because you can't really make any progress.' A third expressed, 'It almost feels like they do it on purpose to avoid paying us bonuses. Only the extreme top performers even qualify for bonuses and their bosses have to make a case for that. But who can get there when you are on your fourth boss in a year? Several of my colleagues left for another company and I'm on my second interview there.'

We've tried to communicate these concerns to him but he is convinced his way is right and the company is doing well financially. Unless things change, we will continue to lose our best people, and it's going to catch up with us eventually because it will be harder to recruit new folks in."

While this example might seem extreme, it's more common than you might think, especially in fast-moving industries or organizations in high-growth mode. In the case above, the leader is driving the constant reorganization. But even when you have a more effective leader, today's job tenures tend to be short, so most departments experience turnover even if it's easy to replace people who leave.

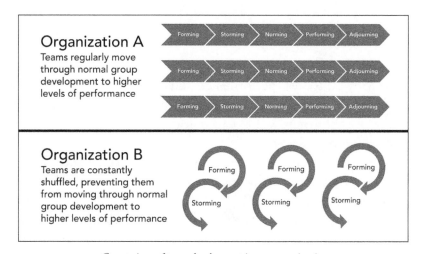

Comparison of team development in two organizations

Organizations that keep teams in a perpetual cycle of forming-storming-norming put them under more stress than ever before, which can lead to unhealthy conflict, ineffective decision-making, and, ultimately, employee disengagement. In addition, the top-performing employees often find this chaos frustrating and unproductive so leave to seek work at more stable organizations.

To avoid this, executives and team leaders have to be more thoughtful and careful about how they help groups come together to work. The best teams intentionally think about how to onboard and integrate new members and allow time for the group to gel. And they engage in team-building and team-training to accelerate the group's development.

5. Dysfunction Emerges

While Tuckman's model paints a picture of a relatively smooth, linear process forward to high performance, today's reality is that things can and often do go off the rails. In fact, the earlier stages determine the trajectory for the group, with the team leader exerting a lot of influence over their future effectiveness.

At the University of Denver, Greg Giesen and Lauri Osborne coauthored a revision of Tuckman's model. They identified that the storming phase is pivotal and sends the group on one of two paths for norming: good or bad. They state, "A team's ability to effectively address and resolve disagreement and conflict will determine whether they move into the good norming or bad norming." The following issues characterize bad norming:

- Team members split off into cliques or factions
- People avoid conflict, either ignoring it or covering it up with false harmony
- Members talk *about* teammates but not directly to the person
- Members who raise concerns about the state of the group are ignored or told to "just deal with it"
- Team leaders are either unaware of the problems or chalk concerns up to personality differences

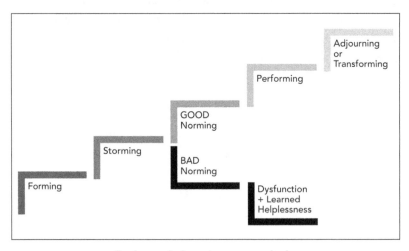

Good versus bad norming as groups develop

While a group can recover from bad norming, it takes focused and intentional effort on the part of the leader to move the group into new patterns of engagement and interaction. This becomes harder the longer the group is allowed to stay in bad norming, as patterns become intractable and members experience what scholars call "learned helplessness," which is essentially giving up on trying to change or even hoping for something better.

Case Study: Financial Services Firm
Org Size: Medium

"I have been in my role for two years. I was tasked to rebuild the learning and development team, which included transitioning out four members while adding new headcount. We grew from 10 to 17, currently. We have a mix of strong skills with limited industry knowledge and subject matter expertise (SME) in finance with minimum facilitation and instructional design skills.

The constant flux of new team members and transition of some long-term team members has caused us to spend more time in forming/storming and it's been hard to get to norming/performing. In this two-year period we've redesigned all of our functional training, launched a professional development series, and a leadership development program for frontline to VP, and began doing talent reviews at the senior level across the enterprise. We've been fully staffed for a solid six months now and are raising the bar on performance expectations and behavior.

There have been three employees along the way who had some polarizing behaviors that contributed to a negative dynamic. Employee #1 is a true business SME, but has a 'been there done that' attitude. Has ability to deliver quantity but not quality. Is passive aggressive and usually at the crux of infighting. We have let this go on too long. E#2: was aggressive to colleagues and was terminated after 60 days. E#3: Super creative, amazing technical skills, lacked focus and ability to stay consistent. Lots of love/hate from teammates given inability to deliver results consistently.

At the end of the day, the leadership (me) sets the tone and reinforces the team vibe. I have been working to be more cognizant of our dynamic, spend more time individually with team members (difficult given I have 12 direct reports), and more time in the group talking about team formation, getting to know each other and understanding each other's strengths in action, both

---

positive and negative. I have focused on using my own emotions to set the tone. This has included being clear when disappointed and being more mindful of sending positive messages as well."

Dysfunctional norms cripple teams in every industry around the world. Patrick Lencioni, a leading expert on teams in organizations, identified five common dysfunctions in his book *The Five Dysfunctions of a Team*. The first is the absence of trust, which emerges because the fear of being vulnerable gets in the way. The second is fear of conflict because members attempt to preserve a sense of harmony that actually stifles normal and productive conflict. The third is lack of commitment because members either never had clarity about or fully bought into the goals and process. As a result, they can't make decisions they can stick to. The fourth is avoidance of accountability because members are too uncomfortable with each other to hold each other responsible for their behaviors and performance. The final dysfunction is inattention to results because members are pursuing their own goals and status rather than collective success.

Lencioni's five dysfunctions of a team

Teams that experience even one of these dysfunctions are at risk for failing to accomplish their goals as well as driving disengagement and attrition. And since dysfunctions can cascade, it's common for teams to experience several, even up to all five.

6. Collaboration, Coordination, and Cooperation

As teams work together, they are often asked to move back and forth along a continuum of complexity. This requires them to understand the difference between coordination, cooperation, and collaboration and to appropriately engage in each at the right time.

As I dug into the data, I found many different and disparate definitions of these common words we use every day in our workplaces. I explored several sources and found them all helpful, yet wanting. Many were written by academic scholars who may not experience the typical issues of the daily work done in business, government, and nonprofit sectors. As a result, I synthesized the elements into a new model that more accurately reflects how work is done in real workplaces around the world. Let's look at the definitions and differences:

1. **Coordination** is the orchestrated efforts of individuals or groups, to align or synchronize *separate* actions. They exchange relevant information and resources in support of each other's distinct goals. In other words, people *co-ordinate* (align/sync) distinct efforts (such as IT upgrading computers and facilities changing out desks) to create more efficiency, but they remain independent.

2. **Cooperation** is the coordinated efforts of a group of two or more people to perform their assigned portion of an agreed-upon *shared process or task*. They are dependent on each other to execute a mutual objective. People *co-operate* to perform their portion of a shared task, as planned. For example, IT works with Finance and Shipping to ensure that new computers are purchased and delivered on time.

3. **Collaboration** is the mutual engagement of a group of two or more in a cocreative effort that achieves a *shared goal or vision*. They are interdependent, with each unique contribution essential to the whole. People *co-labor* in an act of creation, and the result is changed by the input of all the contributors. An example would be several people and departments working together to shift an organization's culture.

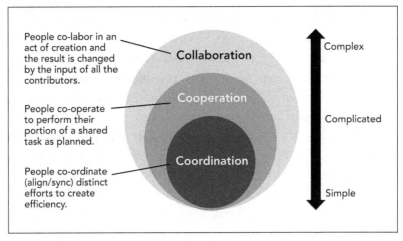

Levels of work done by teams

Collaboration is a vital necessity for the success of today's organizations and yet is probably the least understood skill. I hear the word "collaboration" often in my work with organizations around the world. But people often use the term when they actually mean cooperation or coordination.

Collaboration is a special act of cocreation, and the outcomes are often both unpredictable and impossible to achieve without the individual contributions of every member. The author of *The Collaborative Instinct*, Jelenko Dragisic, puts it this way, "If collaboration does not change you, then you are not collaborating. Collaboration does not come about without some kind of organizational enlightenment."

I have found that instead of these being three distinct types of work, collaboration is an umbrella containing cooperation and coordination within it. Some groups and teams may only operate in one or two zones on a daily basis. But more and more, teams are being asked to move across the levels seamlessly.

This means that teams often must switch back and forth between goals, intentions, and skill sets, which can be difficult when our work blends together over the course of our daily schedule. We might be in a meeting at 9 a.m. to coordinate with another department, then go right into another meeting where we must cooperate with two other groups, followed by a working project session that is all about collaboration.

Coordination only requires basic communication and planning skills (though many people still struggle with this), but cooperation requires a clear process for execution and accountability, and collaboration requires the most advanced skills of all: building trust, engaging in creativity and innovation, and having a mindful process for resolving the inevitable conflict that arises from this most complex form of work.

	Coordination	Cooperation	Collaboration
What	People co-ordinate (align/sync) distinct efforts to create efficiency.	People co-operate to perform their portion of a shared task, as planned.	People co-labor in an act of creation and the result is changed by the input of all the contributors.
Definition	The orchestrated efforts of individuals or groups to align or synchronize separate actions. They exchange relevant information and resources in support of each other's distinct goals.	The coordinated efforts of a group of two or more people to perform their assigned portion of an agreed-upon shared process or task. They are dependent on each other to execute a mutual objective.	The mutual engagement of a group of two or more in a cocreative effort that achieves a shared goal or vision. They are interdependent with each unique contribution essential to the whole.
Goal	Align/synchronize efforts.	Execute assigned portion of shared process.	Achieve shared vision through cocreation.
How	Effective communication ensures efficiency.	Smooth process drives execution. An expected task is achieved as planned.	Creative tension drives innovation. Something new is created as a result.

Yet, I have found that most organizations do not offer the right learning and training to help teams develop the skills they need to perform successfully at these various levels. Plus, team leaders are often chosen because they were excellent performers or individual contributors, which does not make them qualified to create a collaborative environment. In fact, research has found that the best individual performers often *don't* make effective team leaders because they inevitably and unconsciously use the team to execute their own vision rather than harnessing the strengths of others to cocreate something new.

It's vital that organizations choose team leaders based on their skills for creating the environment for *others* to collaborate. This includes the new leader making the critical pivot from performer to facilitator, so they help others develop trust, engage with respect, resolve conflict, and wrestle with the often challenging work of creativity and innovation. It turns out the best team leaders have what is called collaborative intelligence or CQ. Collaborative intelligence is the ability to think with others, valuing the diverse ways people frame questions, process information, and innovate new ideas. No surprise, the best team members also have CQ.

As Dr. Dawna Markova and Angie McArthur, authors of *Collaborative Intelligence: Thinking with People Who Think Differently* write, "Leaders who understand and maximize the different ways that people process information are more prepared to inspire, empower, and meld the diverse intellectual assets within their organizations." Effective team leaders know they have a responsibility to create the environment and conditions for a diverse group of members to come together to do the difficult but rewarding work of collaboration.

Thinking back on Tuckman's model, we can then begin to understand that "performing" includes different *kinds* of performing. For some groups it involves coordination; for others it is both coordination and cooperation. But in many groups today—those tasked with moving their organizations forward in significant ways—it's about collaborating.

This book focuses on that highest level of complexity, because I know from my work with all kinds of organizations that collaboration is where the real important and strategic work lives. It's also where teams struggle the most.

I believe that is because we are working against (rather than with) human biology and I have found some compelling and astounding answers in studying the neuroscience of teams. Neurobiology drives how we work together at our best and when we perform at our worst.

Your Learning Journey

Take a few minutes to reflect on your own experiences on teams over the past few years.

- Think about how your team progressed through Tuckman's stages of forming, storming, norming, performing, and adjourning/transforming. Did your group exhibit the hallmark behaviors? How long did you spend in each stage?
- Reflect on times you experienced both good and bad norming. What differentiated the two experiences? What do you think set you on one path versus the other?

- Identify which of Lencioni's five dysfunctions of a team you have experienced and when.
- Review the difference between coordination and collaboration. How might this distinction help you perform better on teams you are currently a part of?

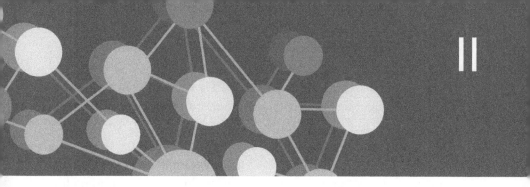

THE BRAIN SCIENCE
OF GROUPS & TEAMS

"Teams naturally reach high performance in three to five years. But get this right and you can fast track it to as little as six months. Understanding how the brain works literally accelerates everything."

Zane Harris, NeuroPower Group

7. The Brain During Good Norming and Performing

In my research of the neuroscience of teams, I discovered that our brains are designed to help us become more connected and effective in groups. As best-selling author and researcher Dr. Brené Brown states, "If there's one thing I know for sure, it's that we are wired for connection." In fact, our survival as a species depends on it. Our tribal ancestors had to work together every day, building shelter, finding food, and defending themselves from danger. Let's look closer to see what's happening when we are at our best when working in groups.

The brain science of teams is a new field because the medical technology has only recently evolved. MRI machines accommodate only one person, not a group. Even if you could stuff a team in there, it would be difficult for people to replicate realistic work interactions.

Fortunately, researchers are using new technologies and methods for seeing into human brains as we engage with each other in real time. The fMRI (functional magnetic resonance imaging) is still a key tool, and researchers can link several people in different MRI machines so they can communicate, problem-solve, and interact. Despite the fact that this research is happening in artificial lab settings, it still provides exciting new insights.

To observe more realistic situations, researchers are using complex headsets and caps loaded with sensors that can detect activity in regions all around the brain. Each member of the group or team wears these devices while working together and the data is captured in real time allowing researchers to see minute-by-minute shifts.

The electro-encephalogram (EEG), transcranial magnetic stimulation (TMS), and functional near-infrared spectroscopy (fNIRS) are tools that help us see which regions or structures of the brain are active and also record and compare the brain waves of each participant.

Scientists have long known that different regions of our brain control different functions. And they can detect which region is active by measuring a variety of indicators, including electrical pulses, light absorption, and glucose burn. New technologies now allow us to see which regions of a person's brain are activate while they are engaging or interacting with others: which lobe of the brain is activated, and even which brain structure, cluster of neurons, or individual neuron is firing.

Brain activity can also be seen through brain waves, which are created from the electrical pulses as neurons communicate with each other. Like sound waves or radio signals, brain waves are measured based on how fast they oscillate. Brain waves range on a continuum of six speeds from very low (infralow at <.5HZ) to very fast (gamma at 38–42HZ). Each wave pattern indicates different states of alertness.

- **Infralow (<.5HZ):** Not much is known about these slow oscillating brainwaves because they are difficult to detect and measure. However, scientists believe they play a role in network function and timing as well as very advanced states of meditation.

- **Delta (.5–3HZ):** These waves are similar to a slow drum beat, loud and penetrating. Scientists observe them during deep meditation, detached awareness, and dreamless sleep, where they stimulate healing and regeneration.

- **Theta (3–8HZ):** Theta waves also are present during sleep and meditation but more at the edges of waking. Scientists have found associations with learning, memory, and intuition as well as vivid imagery and information outside our normal conscious awareness.

- **Alpha (8–12HZ):** Alpha waves are the hallmark of the resting but awake brain during quiet contemplation or some meditative states. Scientists believe they help with relaxation,

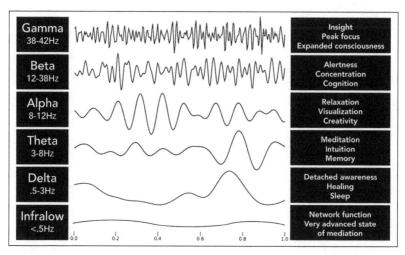

Different levels of brain waves

visualization, creativity, mind-body integration, and mental coordination.

- **Beta (12–38HZ):** An awake and alert brain exhibits one of three levels of beta waves. Low beta (12–15HZ) is considered a musing state. Beta (15–22HZ) occurs when we are actively figuring something out, and high beta (22–38HZ) is the hallmark of complex thought, excitement or anxiety.

- **Gamma (38–42HZ):** These are the fastest-oscillating waves and occur when the brain is processing information from several different areas simultaneously. The mind has to be quiet to access this level, not actively thinking. Gamma waves are involved with insight, peak focus, and expanded consciousness. They are highly active when we're in engaged in behaviors like universal love and altruism.

Brain waves can be visualized on screens or paper, allowing researchers to overlay several people's signals to analyze similarities and differences.

Together, these methods of brain analysis have opened up a whole new phase of research into the science of human interaction, particularly in regard to groups and teams. Let's walk through some key studies and findings and then I'll tie them together with some takeaways for how we help teams thrive.

8. Neural Synchrony

It turns out that our brains are designed to do something scientists call neural synchrony or entrainment. Engaging with each other can align our brains to each other, aiding our ability to communicate and interact productively. When conditions are right and we achieve this synchrony, our thoughts and behaviors drive enhanced understanding, effectiveness, and efficiency, even across cultural differences and distance.

Princeton professor Dr. Uri Hasson is a neuroscientist who studies human communication, particularly how meaning is conveyed between people and among groups. He looked at two specific aspects of the brain: which regions of the brain are activated during communication and how this impacts brain waves.

Dr. Hasson and his team did a series of experiments that uncovered some surprising findings when studying participants on an fMRI scanner telling or listening to real-life stories. First, they discovered that during communication the same regions of our brain light up—even across a wide range of listeners—showing neural synchrony among them. Participants' brain waves, which were quite different before a story began, actually aligned, showing a nearly identical wave pattern. In other words, the various listeners experienced wave synchrony.

Hasson's team went further, to explore the cause of the synchrony: Was it just the brain responding to the sounds of a voice? Or the words of spoken language? Or the meaning the speaker was trying to convey?

By playing a story backwards, the auditory complex was still activated in all the listeners, but not the other regions, because the story became just sounds with no recognizable language or meaning. When they took a story and turned it into a scramble of words and bits of sentences, the subjects showed neural synchrony in the language centers of the brain.

When the story was intact and in order, more regions of the brain lit up, including higher-order thinking areas in the frontal and parietal cortexes. This occurred when speakers conveyed meaning through their stories and the neural synchrony across all the listeners was quite significant.

They then took the study one step further, which was to take the exact same story and replicate the study with both an English speaker and listeners as well as a Russian speaker and listeners. In other words, the sounds and language are different but the meaning is the same.

And guess what? All of the listeners experienced neural synchrony even across cultural and language differences. Dr. Hasson believes this is because we have what he calls "a common code that presents meaning."

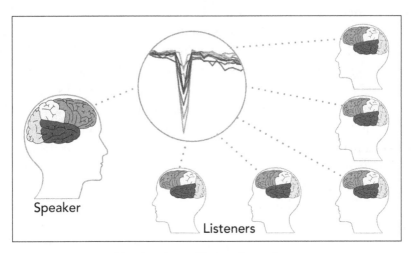

Neural synchrony of brain regions and waves

The Princeton researchers also explored neural synchrony between the speaker and listeners. They expected to find large differences, because talking and telling a story is a very different act than listening and comprehending a story. But they found neural synchrony in both brain regions and brain waves between the speaker and listeners. And, in fact, the greater the neural synchrony or alignment, the better the communication.

Finally, to see if neural synchrony happens over space and time, they studied which parts of participants' brain lit up when participants watched a section of a movie. Researchers asked them to tell others about what they saw and found that the same part of participants' brains lit up when they were describing what they saw as when they were watching the movie. Indicating that when we share a memory, that same part of our brain activates as the original experience.

Even more fascinating, listeners' brains lit up the same way. In other words, it conveyed more than the story's meaning; the neural synchrony allowed them access to the actual experience.

Dr. Matt Lieberman, Director of UCLA's Social Cognitive Neuroscience Lab, is also studying neural synchrony on teams. His group is using functional near infrared spectroscopy (fNIRS) to look for similarities in brain activity across a range of topics. One study looked at how different fighter pilots respond to the same flying conditions. They were able to capture recordings of the pilots' neural activity, using fNIRS headsets, and then do a second-by-second analysis of how the individuals and the group experienced the flight.

Lieberman's team is also looking at how neural synchrony unfolds over typical team meetings, and the kind of things that cause both short- and long-term disruption of the synchrony. He hypothesizes that comments are actions that could be threatening to members, such as a sexist or racist comment, could break the synchrony of the group. At the time of this book's publication, this study had not yet been published so keep an eye on his work to see what he finds.

The UCLA group believes that neural synchrony is more powerful than we realize and can even serve to be predictive. One study, by Dr. Carolyn Parkinson, looked at how neural similarities might predict social networks and friendship. She did a study with college students, recording their neural activity while they watched a variety of videos. She then compared those recordings, looking at 80 different regions of the brain across 861 different pairings. She was able to predict, with 80 percent accuracy, who became friends in real life based on their neural synchrony.

So, what does this all mean for teams? We now know that our brains are designed for neural synchrony and, when we achieve it, communication between people becomes more clear, effective, and connected. You may have experienced this phenomenon. It's when we feel the difference between just understanding someone's words and really "getting it"—knowing or understanding it on a deeper level. We literally feel "in sync."

Neural synchrony can also be a driver of team performance, contributing to faster and better communication, comprehension and, ultimately, quality of work. This can be said of all types of teams; not just those at work, but also our romantic partnerships, family relationships, friendship networks, and neighborhood communities. But as we'll discover in section III, certain conditions can enhance or harm our ability to achieve neural synchrony, especially in work environments.

9. Mirror Neurons

One of the brain's major contributors to communication and connection is our mirror neuron system. Thanks to many conclusive studies we know this once-controversial idea as truth: mirror neurons exist and aid people in with observational learning and empathy.

First discovered in the 1980s by Dr. Giacomo Rizzolatti and other Italian neuroscientists who were studying monkeys, mirror neurons are a class or type of neurons in the brain that fire or light up when we perform an act that has a specific goal. For example, picking up food to feed ourselves or grasping a tool to use it. But it turns out that the same neurons fire when we *observe* someone doing those acts as well, creating an "inner experience" of something we are observing in others.

UCLA neuroscientist, Dr. Marco Iocaboni, has expanded on the research by focusing on humans and various aspects of social connections and how we communicate our intentions and feelings. He writes, "When I see you smiling, my mirror neurons for smiling fire up, too, initiating a cascade of neural activity that evokes the feeling we typically associate with a smile. I don't need to make any inference on what you are feeling, I experience immediately and effortlessly (in a milder form, of course) what you are experiencing."

This is the basis for empathy: the ability to understand or identify with the perspective, experiences, and motivations of another person and to comprehend and share another person's emotional state. Empathy is different than sympathy, which is caring for the suffering of others but from a separate, more distant place. Sympathy is feeling sorry *for* you while empathy is feeling your pain *with* you.

You may have experienced this when a colleague has laughed and you found yourself laughing too, or when a friend has cried and you teared up as well. Mirror neurons are also at play when we see someone get hurt or injured and we feel that clench in our belly.

Dr. Iocaboni went on to publish groundbreaking work on how reduced mirror neuron activity is involved with people with autism, who often struggle with social interactions and correctly identifying emotions in others. He claims that a deficit in mirror neurons is tied to the regions of the brain affiliated with social engagement, language acquisition, and motor skills, the three major symptoms of autism. You can learn more in his book *Mirroring People: The Science of How We Connect to Others.*

Psychologist Christopher Hopwood at Michigan State University has also seen the effect of mirror neurons in how we engage with others. His studies of human behavior have found that humans normally do something called complementary behavior. It means that if you act friendly or open to another person, they are likely to respond similarly back. If you act with rudeness or hostility, you'll likely get that back too.

Mirror neurons are naturally involved with observational learning. Evolutionarily, this helped us pass on useful skills to the next generation, increasing our group's chances of survival. When adults show children how to find food or build a shelter, their mirror neurons play a role in helping the learning stick. This is why demonstration is such an effective and valuable learning strategy. The brain is wired to learn first by watching others and then by doing.

As medical technology has improved, it is now possible to explore how mirror neurons work with groups of people. A group of researchers in Belgium used transcranial magnetic stimulation (TMS) to study whether observing several people would have a stronger effect or impact on a person's mirror neurons than just observing one person.

And in fact, it does. It makes sense that, biologically, our body will respond more strongly to a group of people experiencing the same emotion because that group might be conveying important information for our own survival and well-being. This effect is called group contagion. According to the researchers, "Groups may be more contagious simply because their actions resonate louder."

Mirror neurons have profound implications for teams in today's workplaces. When we work together, we are naturally exposed to each other's feelings, intentions, and actions. Mirror neurons are there, working in the background to help us quickly understand each other. Positive impacts include observational learning and enhanced communication and empathy. Through observation, we can learn from each other, quickening how we gain new skills and competencies. Putting highly skilled members with others could uplevel the group if the right opportunities for observational learning are put in place.

In addition, mirror neurons can help teams convey and comprehend emotions so they experience empathy for each other. Studies have shown that empathy is a core component of creating an environment that is safe for taking risks and making mistakes, something that is a key differentiator for the highest-performing teams (more on this in the next section).

The downside is that the effect of mirror neurons can also hasten a group's decline through contagion. If members are not appropriately skilled, they may learn each other's incompetence or bad habits. In addition, when members of a group are anxious or disengaged, other members are more likely to join them in those negative states. Mirror neurons are operating every day and influencing how we work in pairs and in groups. We need to be mindful of the powerful impact of this system and make sure we support teams so they maximize benefits and minimize potential risks.

Case Study: Research University
Org Size: Large

"Our IT team serves 80 percent of the students by operating computer labs and providing training. Our biggest challenge is a hostile environment created by the director that impacts our ability to work together. Of the 30 people who were there when I started, 15 have quit. We have three main challenges:

1. Unsure of future goals. When we are given a project, we are often not given any real explanation and told to just 'deal with it.' We are rarely assured of the resources we need to accomplish projects. And once we begin working, projects are often pulled without any reason given.

2. Manager is hostile to people who disagree with him. Even if you provide data, he shuts down any ideas he doesn't like. He ostracizes people in public, pushing them 'out of the circle' permanently. It is difficult to form alliances with others as they know that agreeing with you is dangerous to their career health. He regularly yells at employees and has even grabbed one by the arm during a meeting to prevent her from leaving the room.

3. Organization is not responding fast enough. Several employees (eight of us) have formally reported the issue to the Dean and HR, providing documented examples. They spoke with him and now it's worse than ever because he is extremely suspicious of everyone. He has started assassinating people's character loudly in the hallway saying things such as, 'So-and-so apparently went to HR and told them I threatened him. That's not true, isn't that crazy?' Weeks have gone by and nothing seems to be getting better. I have just given my notice."

However real their effects may be, researchers are still not exactly sure how the mirror neuron process happens. They are just now discovering what parts of the brain are involved. Different, physically unconnected parts of the brain can be simultaneously involved in complex processes. Perhaps the signals pass via chemicals or electrical pulses; perhaps they transmit invisibly between people, much like radio waves and cell phone signals transmit data through the air until they reach their receiver. There is no doubt that we are only beginning to discover the many mysteries of the brain.

10. Sense of We and the Rhythm of a Team

Researchers have revealed two other powerful neurological components of effective groups and teams, called the "sense of we" and the "rhythm of a team." Let's explore both.

Over the years, many researchers have studied the concept of self-other merging. But only recently have they been able to explore the neurological components. When we move from being the "self" to being part of a collective or group, we change to the "sense of we." This phenomenon is also affiliated with mirror neurons as well as the medial prefrontal cortex (mPFC) in the brain. It represents a shift from seeing ourselves as individuals to being part of a group. When it happens, we psychologically switch to a sense that we are in this together and it creates the zone for cooperation, which can also create the conditions for the "sense of we." Neuroscientists at the University of Geneva found that setting up a group in a cooperative task influenced their mirror neuron system in different ways than when a similar group was set up in a competitive task. When people were on the same team, their mirror neurons fired more quickly for both successes and errors of their teammates. In contrast, the brains of the people in the competitive group stayed in a self-centered perspective and had slower error-processing responses.

Another study at the University of Amsterdam found similar results. Participants were asked to respond to a stimulus and take action, sometimes alone and sometimes together with another person. Results showed that the fastest groups were those who were in a positive relationship that was friendly and cooperative, outperforming the people who were paired with someone who was intimidating and competitive. This means that teams who are set up to see themselves as part of a group and in a cooperative relationship are likely to perform better and faster because their mirror neuron systems become more attuned and respond more quickly.

The second component is what Dr. Ronald Stevens, a researcher at the UCLA Brain Research Institute, has coined the "rhythm of a team." He has done extensive research on teams who are actively engaged in a complex task, to mimic real conditions for teams in today's workplaces. He and his team explored how neural synchronies develop and change over the course of a project with several members involved.

They used wireless EEG headsets to measure the brain waves of teams engaged in two different complex tasks that involved working together to navigate through obstacles and respond to both anticipated and unexpected challenges. One group included naval officers training for the US Navy's Basic Enlisted Submarine School.

Much like Uri Hasson's studies, the brain waves of the team members were quite different before the tasks began, but once the group started working together, the brain waves came into alignment representing neural synchrony.

Because they were studying subjects working on a changing, complex task, they were able to gather data about what happened within the team members' brains, both individually and collectively, at various points. They found that the tasks had five distinct activities:

- Identifying the problem
- Forming possible solutions
- Sharing ideas
- Converging on one solution
- Dealing with unexpected challenges

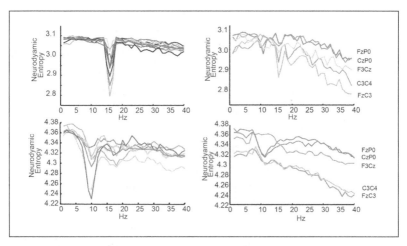

Neural synchrony across several types of tasks

The researchers discovered that each phase of the task had its own unique neural signature that was unlike the other phases. And at each phase the members came into neural synchrony, signaling an observable period of high performance, which would then be lost as the team experienced constraints or challenges that forced them to change their approach.

Stevens calls these periods of adaptive change "neurodynamic reorganizations," stating, "When the challenges in the environmental landscape exceed the base level of complexity for the team's experience, then the overall team rhythm can be lost and the crew must work dynamically to reconfigure their interactions to establish new rhythms matched to the new constraints of the task."

Case Study: Global Tech Company
Org Size: Large

"This team was pulled together as part of an overall change-management strategy for assisting the Americas Operations team through the transition onto a new IT platform. Called the 'Change Agent Team,' leaders asked for volunteers to serve as peer leaders by becoming early adopters of the new systems and processes and help guide their team members in the first few months after the transformation occurred.

Change agents also served as a first line of support for the end users and were coached in techniques of how to best assist employees through the human side of the change process. The change agents formed their own network for peer-to-peer support leveraging collaborative technology such as Spark rooms to encourage knowledge sharing and resolve issues more effectively.

The Senior Director of the Ops team noticed increased collaboration immediately after the go-live of the systems. People were standing up from their desks and asking each other questions like 'Have you encountered this problem? How did you solve it?' The effort required to understand the new process become a team effort through the efforts of the change agent program. No one felt alone.

Having this type of individual contributor be given an elevated status also alleviates the pressure on the managers to be the point person for the entire team during a time of high amounts of change. Employees often feel more comfortable approaching a peer versus a manager if they were struggling with a new process or system. This truly created a network of knowledge sharing that we had never experienced before as an organization.

As a result of this program's success, we have now expanded the concept to not just be tied to this one-time transformation, but

---

all ongoing organizational changes through a long-term strategy of peer leader Ambassadors. The Ambassadors now assist with everything from onboarding of new hires to process improvements training."

Researchers believe that the most effective teams are those that can find their rhythm quickly and respond effectively to disturbances, reestablishing synchrony. It's important to note that neural synchrony is not "group think" where overly cohesive teams ignore information or ideas that might challenge the group's norms or flow. Those are behavioral choices that can be seen by observers. Neural synchrony is an internal state that can only be seen with specialized devices and create a whole new awareness of what peak performance looks like.

We'll discover in chapter 15 that diverse ideas, styles and backgrounds actually drive better team performance when the team has the right skills to utilize them.

11. Team Fractals

One final study caught my attention as I explored research on the neuroscience of teams: Researchers from UCLA, Arizona State, and Texas Tech universities used fractal analysis to look at the neural signatures of teams. Fractals describe dynamic systems and have a spatial or geometric structure that is repeated at various levels of the organism. An example is a tree where the geometry of a trunk splitting off into branches is replicated in the individual leaves with the main stem and veins. Other examples include rivers, seashells, blood vessels, and hurricanes.

Examples of fractals

As those examples show, fractals abound in nature. But they can also be made by humans, using mathematical equations that replicate natural patterns. You'll find them in screensavers, light shows at staged events, and art. A study by Dr. Richard Taylor, a physicist at the University of Oregon, found that Jackson Pollok's paintings contain fractal patterns, perhaps explaining why so many people feel drawn to, and find harmony in, the seemingly chaotic images.

Humans tend to have predictable responses to fractals. We find them soothing, according to EEGs and skin conductivity tests, which measure activity in the nervous system. Taylor's study found that people who viewed fractal patterns that most closely mirror those in nature (known as midrange fractals) recovered from stress 60 percent faster than those viewing other patterns. It also impacted the brain, creating the alpha brainwave pattern that signals a wakeful and relaxed state. This impact even occurred when people viewed the images for only one minute. In fact, these midrange fractals have a similar soothing impact on the brain as music.

Taylor argues that our biological systems exhibit the same midrange fractal pattern. From our blood vessels and neurons to the structures in our eyes, we are a living, breathing example of a natural fractal. So it's not surprising that we find them soothing. As Taylor puts it, "Your visual system is in some way hardwired to understand fractals. The stress-reduction is triggered by a physiological resonance that occurs when the fractal structure of the eye matches that of the fractal image being viewed."

The researchers who used fractal analysis to study teams were exploring another aspect of our human connection to fractals. They argue that teams within organizations replicate the nested nature of other complex and interconnected systems. For example, members of a team working together would mimic the various departments and functions working together but at a different scale, much like the leaf mirrors the tree. They used EEGs to explore the brain patterns of six-person teams completing a complex task, comparing various levels of analysis of the brain wave patterns with observations of the teams' progress and self-reported data from the members themselves.

As in other complex structures, analysis showed that the teams' brain waves exhibited fractal patterns at many levels of scale (think tree branch to leaf vein). They could see the invisible activity of the brain waves emerge to the level of observable social interaction. As they describe it, "The current findings support the conception of teams as highly interconnected, dynamical systems. Given that fractal and multifractal properties are recognized as markers of health in physiological systems (for example, Peng, et al., 1995), those same properties may also be useful in assessing the general 'health' of a team (that is, its adaptability and responsiveness to the changing environment)."

They argue further that fractal analysis might become a useful tool for assessing the health of a team and even predicting periods of dysfunction so they can be addressed.

Combining their findings with Richard Taylor's it's clear that, as individuals, we feel the difference when a team is operating smoothly. I have personally experienced less stress, more pleasure, higher engagement, and more productivity. And I am not alone.

In my consulting work, I can see and feel the difference in the health of the teams I engage with. On a biological level, my body recognizes it before the data confirms it.

These findings underscore what I have been arguing for years: organizations are living ecosystems of biological beings. And that we must treat people and teams in ways that honor our biology, rather than working against it. We'll explore ways to do that in the next section.

So, what does this mean for teams? That we are biologically wired to work in groups and our brains are designed to align with others to create more effective communication, connection, and collaboration. And, in fact, this is what we see unfolding with high-performing teams. They find that neural synchrony quickly, learn by watching each other, naturally extend empathy, and realign effectively when challenges or barriers arise.

But if we're wired for this, why are teams failing in record numbers and spectacular ways? Because *other* aspects of our biology are even stronger and, when triggered, make it physically impossible for us to perform at our best. We'll explore this more in the next section.

Your Learning Journey

Reflect on your own experiences, past and current, with the brain science of teams.

- Identify times when you think you have experienced neural synchrony with others, both in your professional and personal life. What was the experience like for you?
- How might you leverage the mirror neuron system to aid in observational learning and empathy on a team?
- Consider times when a team leader did a good job of creating a sense of we on your team. What did they do and say, specifically, that helped build that connection?

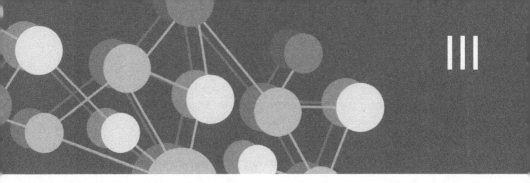

THE BRAIN SCIENCE OF
SAFETY & BELONGING

"Psychological safety is a sense of confidence that the team will not embarrass, reject, or punish someone for speaking up with ideas, questions, concerns, or mistakes. It is a shared belief that the team is safe for interpersonal risk-taking. It describes a team climate characterized by interpersonal trust and mutual respect in which people are comfortable being themselves."

Dr. Amy Edmondson, Harvard Business School,
Teaming: How Organizations Learn, Innovate and Compete in the Knowledge Economy

Here's the good news: we are wired to work together in groups and teams. And when it goes well, we get smooth-running, high-performing teams: productive, efficient, and innovative. That's "good" norming and peak performing at its best. But "bad" norming can easily happen too, sending the group into an ongoing struggle of dysfunction. What sets groups on one path versus the other is what happens in the forming and storming phases.

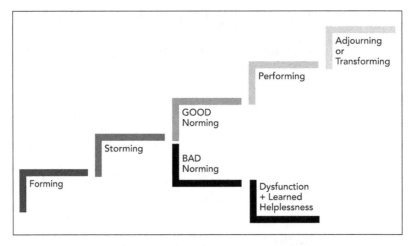

Forming and storming phases determine the two paths of norming

When members are getting to know each other and engaging in that initial conflict, it can be healthy *if* some very critical elements get established that determine the trajectory going forward. And brain science is at play here too. It turns out that while we are wired to connect with others, there are some prerequisites. These are safety, belonging, inclusion, and trust.

Safety
Our biology is powerful. When you look at all the structures in our systems, it becomes clear that our species is wired for three key things:

1. **To survive.** This is our need for food, water, and shelter. Recent global conflicts and natural disasters like hurricanes have highlighted how primal these needs are. People will go to extraordinary lengths to gain and protect food, water, and shelter because of our most basic need to stay alive.

When we are not in crisis, these needs come in the form of job security because earning a paycheck is how we purchase food and shelter. So anything that messes with our sense of job security, like a new boss, a performance review, or being assigned to a new team, can trigger these primal instincts.

2. **To belong.** This is our need to be part of a community and form meaningful bonds with others. This is tightly interwoven with our need to survive because our chances of survival are greater when we are part of a tribe. Entire structures of our anatomy are dedicated to helping us understand and connect with others. Emotionally, we are driven to find connections. We hunger for and seek a place to belong and we are sensitive to our place within the group because, biologically, we know that leaving a group can be dangerous.

3. **To become.** Once the other two needs are met, our final and perhaps greatest need is to become our best selves—to grow into our potential and make the contribution we are here to make. This is the "seeking" part of human nature and it distinguishes us from all the other living organisms on the planet. Our brains are wired to seek new levels of growth and structures dedicated to creating feelings of reward or success to steer us away from failure.

Some of you may recognize this as a simplified version of Maslow's hierarchy of human needs, and it is. While Maslow identified five levels, I have found that collapsing them into these three categories give us both clarity and a sense of priority that aligns with how issues play out in today's workplaces.

Working in teams is related to all three core human needs. Being on a team can enhance or threaten our sense of job security. Working with others creates an additional community to belong to or feel excluded from. And, often, our work in teams is tied to our desire to reach our fullest potential through our professional growth and development.

Again, this is why teams are perhaps the single most important entity in today's workplace: When we get them right, we leverage so many powerful aspects of human biology that can propel both individuals and the organization forward. But getting it wrong can cripple an organization's ability to be competitive or succeed.

The Triune Brain…Then and Now

Our need to survive, belong, and become are such core functions of our biology that our brains have structures and processes dedicated to each, and they influence each other. One way to understand this is through concept of the triune brain, first proposed in 1960 by Dr. Paul MacLean, a physician and neuroscientist at Yale Medical School. He believed that the brain operates in three layers.

The innermost or core level is known as the reptilian brain and contains the structures that drive our basic living functions like heart rate, breathing, and temperature—things of which we have no conscious control. Also, part of this level is our survival responses of fight-flight-freeze, which is controlled by the amygdala. The amygdala is fed by all the major sensory nerves and constantly scans for danger, which includes scanning for change as this can be a warning sign for danger. Called the survival or reptilian brain, MacLean argues that all living creatures share this core level.

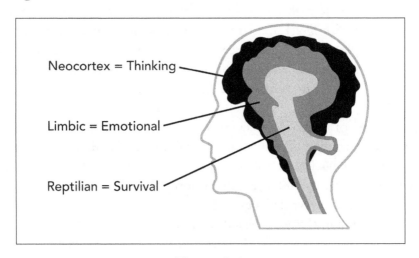

The triune brain

The second layer is called the limbic or emotional brain. MacLean argues that this layer holds our core emotions like joy, anger, fear, sadness, disgust, etc., and is shared by all mammals. This is why we can see recognizable emotions in our pet dogs and cats as well as cows, pigs, and sheep. If you have ever had a dog you have probably witnessed the sheer explosion of joy they show when you walk through the door or they find a dead squirrel to roll in (eewww!). It's also why animal rights activists work so hard to create better protections for animals in the food industry.

Finally, the outermost layer is the neocortex or thinking brain. MacLean purports that this layer holds our higher-level thinking skills like logical analysis and reason, which is what distinguishes us from the rest of the animals, except cetaceans like whales and dolphins who share this third layer. Here is where we find more subtle and nuanced emotions as well as the ability to organize ourselves into societies with norms, rules, and laws. This is also where our self-awareness lives.

Several scholars have found that these layers influence each other and that when we are in a survival situation, the reptilian brain takes over, essentially shutting down the higher layers. For example, when we are under threat or are injured, resources are efficiently diverted in our bodies to help us survive. Hormones are released to aid speed, strength, and physical recovery of potential injuries, and our self-awareness goes offline to protect us from shock.

UCLA neuroscientist Dr. Matt Lieberman has found that when the rational brain is no longer in control, we lose 50 to 75 percent of our mental capacity. We literally lose access to our intelligence, reducing us to about 25 percent as smart as we really are.

While modern research and technology have disproved some of McLean's assertions, there's still value in the general concept. For example, several brain structures span more than one layer and can function across the categories that MacLean describes. While this debunks the notion that the brain is clearly separated into segments like a layer cake, a wide range of scientists still agree that the concept as a whole has merit as a useful way for the general population to understand our brains. Here are the takeaways I find most helpful in my own work and research:

- The brain has different core functions with assigned structures and processes.
- These functions align with Maslow's model and our need to survive, belong, and become.
- Issues of survival and belonging must be handled before we can access the highest levels of our potential.

13. Safety on Teams

Obviously, people need to feel safe on teams. In environments where people are physically aggressive or intimidating, a team will never hit its fullest potential because members will be in their reptilian or survival brains a lot of the time, without access to their higher-thinking abilities, including innovation and creativity. As discussed in the previous chapter, research has shown that even being paired with an intimidating and competitive person negatively impacts performance levels.

Many of us think that physical safety at work is a given these days, but workplace violence and aggression are surprisingly prevalent, both among peers and between supervisors and employees. According to the National Safety Council, every year two million Americans are the victims of workplace violence. About 16 percent of workplace deaths are the result of an attack in the workplace. The National Institute for Occupational Safety and Health analyzes the source of all kinds of workplace injuries and have identified four types of workplace violence:
1. Criminal intent (such as a burglary)
2. Customer and/or client
3. Worker on worker
4. Personal relationships, where the greatest number of victims are women

Some industries are more prone to workplace violence than others. It's the third leading cause of death for healthcare workers, and taxi drivers are twenty times more likely to be murdered on the job than any other worker. Men are the most likely victims at 83 percent of workplace homicides. I was shocked to learn that over one-quarter (26.1 percent) of workplace homicide victims work in sales or retail, higher than those in protective services (19.1 percent) including police officers and security guards.

Of course, we have all seen the damage done by active shooters in the workplace, often injuring or killing several people within minutes. In fact, intentional shooting is the most common mode of workplace homicide (76.2 percent), followed by stabbing (9.7 percent), and beating/shoving (6.2 percent). Nonfatal violent crimes also plague workplaces with the most common crimes being simple assaults (81.5 percent) and aggravated assaults (14.6 percent) followed by rape (1.9 percent) and robbery (1.7 percent).

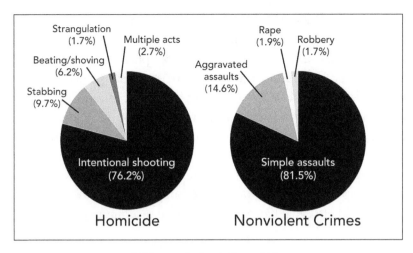

Violence and crime in the workplace

From this data, it's clear that for many, physical safety on the job is a valid and present concern. But separate from potential harm, our sense of physical safety also depends on keeping our job, as our paycheck is the way we buy food, water, and shelter—the essentials of survival. So threatening to fire someone can have nearly the same emotional impact as threatening to hit them, launching a person into the fight-flight-freeze response. Several studies have shown that the amygdala is active during standard work performance reviews, signaling just how threatening the experience can seem.

But perhaps the biggest aspect of safety in today's workplaces is what is called psychological safety. Dr. Amy Edmondson, a professor at the Harvard Business School who studies effective teams, coined this term. She found that, across industries, psychological safety is the key element that differentiates the highest-performing teams from the rest.

Many people face not only a lack of psychological safety at work but they suffer through daily intimidation and fear. *Forbes* featured the research of Dr. Judy Blando, which suggests that 75 percent of workers have been affected by workplace bullying, either as a target or a witness. According to the Workplace Bullying Institute, "workplace bullying" is repeated, health-harming mistreatment of one or more persons (the targets) by one or more perpetrators. It is abusive conduct that is

- threatening, humiliating, or intimidating, or
- work interference (sabotage) that prevents work from getting done, or
- verbal abuse.

It is characterized by regular repetition, ongoing duration, escalation with increasing aggression, intent to harm, and disparity in power. In their national survey, WBI found that 27 percent of employees had been victims of workplace bullying, 21 percent had witnessed bullying happen in their workplace, and another 23 percent was aware it was happening. The targets of the bullying are often the top performers, who bullies presumably find threatening. The report states, "WBI research findings and conversations with thousands of targets have confirmed that targets appear to be the veteran and most skilled person in the group." Alarmingly, workplace bullying is *four times* more common than either sexual harassment or racial discrimination on the job.

Case Study: Private University
Org Size: Large

"The five-person training team designs and develops curricula for a wide range of topics, developing training guides, job aids, webinars, and online learning videos, as well as delivering classroom training. They had been successfully accomplishing the goals and purpose of the team when a new director was hired into a position that had been vacant for nine months.

The director's background is in project management and she does not have experience in training. She makes decisions that reflect superficial or inaccurate knowledge of training and is not willing to trust the experienced team members.

The director's style is rather dictatorial, and she asks the team to produce work that goes against both industry best-practices as well as what has led to success in the past. At first, the team tried to offer input and suggestions, but she seemed easily threatened by these attempts. She labeled one team member's recommendations as an 'act of insubordination' in a performance evaluation. The team is now hiding in their cubicles to avoid missteps and acquiescing to the director's ideas in order to keep their jobs.

The team feels browbeaten, threatened, and intimidated. There is now a hostile work environment that has killed team morale and no longer fosters creativity and innovation. Over the course of ten months, four of the five team members have departed."

But psychological safety is not the mere absence of intimidation or harassment. Dr. Edmondson's research showed that it's what creates the climate for teams to do their *best* work. She defines psychological safety as, "a sense of confidence that the team will not embarrass, reject, or punish someone for speaking up with ideas, questions, concerns, or mistakes. It is a shared belief that the team is safe for interpersonal risk-taking. It describes a team climate characterized by interpersonal trust and mutual respect in which people are comfortable being themselves." You can learn more by watching her TEDx talk or her course on LinkedIn Learning/Lynda.com.

The success of the group and the larger organization often depend on people's ability to speak up, noting potential threats to the group's or organization's success. In fact, in Edmondson's study, the highest-performing teams also had the highest reporting rates for errors. This might seem paradoxical but it's actually the sign of a very healthy team. When people feel safe enough to mention their errors it means they are also holding themselves accountable, and the whole group benefits from learning from the experience, which supports the team's success. In addition, when errors are acknowledged, they can be addressed and fixed, rather than ignored to fester into bigger problems later.

Yet, the reality is that many people stay quiet for fear of being embarrassed, rejected, or punished. If you review recent headlines it's likely you will find stories where someone stayed silent and the consequences were devastating or even fatal. In the investigation following the Columbia Shuttle disaster, it became clear that NASA harbored a culture where employees did not feel comfortable raising concerns to their supervisors (Edmondson features court transcripts in her book *Teaming*). This type of unhealthy team can be found in workplaces of all kinds from operating rooms to boardrooms.

For this reason, psychological safety is especially important—I would argue crucial—for all teams but especially those operating in high levels of uncertainty and whose members are interdependent.

Charles Duhigg, the author of *The Power of Habit*, detailed the significance of psychological safety in his 2016 article for the *New York Times*. He recounts the findings from Google's Project Aristotle, a massive global study of their teams and what distinguishes the best from the average and poor. They replicated Edmondson's findings, discovering that psychological safety was more important than any other factor including the quality or performance level of the individual members. Specifically, they discovered that the best teams did two things: they engaged with each other in a consistent practice of empathy, and ensured that every member was heard. This went beyond inviting people to share their thoughts, to actively seeking out every member's contributions.

Dr. Edmondson calls this behavior "teaming," a different way of engaging with each other that enables and empowers teams to do their best work, with the help of strong leadership. I like that it moves the word team from being a noun to a verb, something that every member participates in.

In addition, Edmondson notes that the leader must actively create psychological safety because their position of power or status naturally suppresses a group's ability to speak up. Effective leaders take intentional steps to invite opinions, ideas, challenges, and critiques.

When training team leaders and managers I emphasize that the ability to create psychological safety is the most important skill they need to have. Yet most people don't even know what it is, let alone how to create it. And we certainly are not measuring teams or their leaders for their efforts in this area. But we should. We'll explore this more in section VI.

It's important to note that psychological safety is not about being universally liked by others, or protected from opinions or beliefs that you find uncomfortable. Again, Edmondson's definition defines psychological safety as "a sense of confidence that the team will not embarrass, reject, or punish someone for speaking up with ideas, questions, concerns, or mistakes. It is a shared belief that the team is safe for interpersonal risk-taking." In other words, the group won't penalize someone for speaking up. Period. They might still disagree, and might find what others say incredibly uncomfortable, but a healthy team welcomes the input and feedback because it might just be the game changer for success.

To continue Edmondson's definition of psychological safety, "It describes a team climate characterized by interpersonal trust and mutual respect in which people are comfortable being themselves." Again, there is nothing here about being liked or popular—it's about respecting and trusting people *at work*, which is about finding value in what they contribute to the group's efforts and being able to count on them because they are reliable.

14. The Drive for Belonging

Psychological safety operates as the bridge between surviving and belonging. Belonging is a core human need that drives many of our behaviors and desires. We all have a deep hunger to belong because to belong is to matter. Belonging enhances the meaning of life and fuels many of our deepest emotions.

University of Kentucky's Dr. C. Nathan DeWall claims, "Humans have a fundamental need to belong. Just as we have needs for food and water, we also have needs for positive and lasting relationships. This need is deeply rooted in our evolutionary history and has all sorts of consequences for modern psychological processes."

It's important to note that belonging is not fitting in. Dr. Brené Brown, author of several best-selling books including *Daring Greatly* and *Rising Strong*, states, "Fitting in is the greatest barrier to belonging. Fitting in is assessing situations and groups of people, then twisting yourself into a human pretzel in order to get them to let you hang out with them. Belonging is something else entirely—it's showing up and letting yourself be seen and known as you really are."

In other words, belonging requires some vulnerability. It takes courage to be authentic because we risk rejection, ridicule, and even harm. Psychological safety is the antidote to this, which is why it has proven to be such a game changer in the workplace.

As with survival, belonging is rooted in several brain structures and processes. We are wired to connect with others. Belonging to a meaningful community translates to physical safety, emotional connection, and even love and continuing the species. Several studies have shown that being connected to others is a source of happiness and longevity. It is also where we can find elements of becoming, because connecting to and helping others gives us a sense of purpose.

What is the brain science of belonging? It's actually somewhat linear, as our brains start processing for connection the moment we come into contact with another person. Doctors Mina Cikara and Jay Van Bavel synthesized the relevant research in their article titled "The Neuroscience of Intergroup Relations: An Integrative Review." Let's look at the four key elements of this fascinating and complex process.

1. Perceive Others' Faces

When we encounter another human, three areas of our brain begin operating to perform what is called face perception. This happens so quickly, in around 200 milliseconds, that we are not conscious of it; but inside our skulls a lot is happening. According to Dr. Marlene Behrmann of Carnegie Mellon University, the brain areas involved with face perception are the fusiform face area (FFA), the occipital face area (OFA), and the superior temporal sulcus (StS). Together, they quickly scan the face with individual neurons responsible for identifying facial geometry as well as specific regions of the face like eyes, nose, eyebrows, cheeks, and hair. In this complex process, scanning happens simultaneously with all the regions working at the same time.

Winrich Freiwald and Doris Tsao have been able to insert audio probes into the brains of monkeys and have even heard the sounds that the neurons make when they fire (kkkrrrr!). Through this process they discovered that the neurons are not groups or clusters dedicated to the eyes or ears, but rather many individual neurons, often microns apart, firing as they scan different areas of our face. Tsao states, "You can have neighboring cells, cells separated by microns, doing totally separate things." These same neurons stayed quiet when other objects were viewed, indicating that they are solely dedicated to face perception.

This part of our biology is incredibly important as it helps us navigate through the thousands of people we will meet or see in our lifetimes. When this aspect of the brain doesn't work, people suffer from a condition called prosopagnosia, a devastating condition where they can't recognize anyone, ever, not even themselves in the mirror. Needless to say, this creates extra anxiety and most sufferers avoid social interactions.

Several studies have shown that the face regions are more active for people we have previously met. Dr. Maria Gobbini at Princeton University found that our brain quickly identifies if we "know" a person, and the regions are more active for familiar faces because the memory areas of the brain are also activated.

All the studies found that activity was happening is several of the face-patch areas, signifying communication between them; however, they have not yet discovered how that occurs. Kerry Grens, author of the article "A Face to Remember," writes "Face perception operates like an orchestra, with units cooperating, communicating, and building upon one another to provide a harmonious picture of facial identity."

2. Scan for Danger: Are You Friend or Foe?

Researchers at the University Medical Center of Geneva, Switzerland, have found that, nearly simultaneously, other regions of the brain scan for whether we could be in possible danger. Dr. Pascal Vrticka and his colleagues explored this process using data from fMRI scans and eye tracking during a series of interactions between participants.

They found that our brain sorts people into one of two categories: friend or foe. This categorization occurs as a combination of reading intent in the moment as well as activating memory for previous interactions with the person. The amygdala, our brain's first responder, is the area responsible. It constantly scans for potential threats, using data it receives from all the major sensory nerves. It looks for signs of threat by searching for emotions and intent in the approaching person's face and body language. Again, the process occurs within milliseconds and without our conscious knowledge, but this aspect of our biology plays a key role in our ability to survive. Detecting potential harm quickly can mean the difference between life and death.

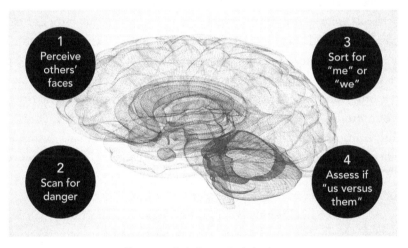

Four neurological scans for belonging

In addition, they found that these initial impressions carry over into future interactions, with the ventral anterior cingulate cortex (VACC) activated when seeing people previously perceived as foes.

Obviously, the biological purpose of this friend/foe sort is to know whether we need to gear up for defense or we can relax. Milliseconds matter and our survival depends on this process. Setting makes a difference too. If you have ever been in a new city, especially at night, you can probably feel your body on high alert. As you get more familiar with the area, you may find things that seemed potentially threatening at first are completely ordinary. When you are at work with lots of people you have known for a while, this part of your biology simmers down because our brain uses the data it already has on our peers. This data-bank of information helps us save energy so we don't prepare to fight when it's unnecessary. But it never completely goes offline. If a trusted coworker entered the room with an aggressive posture or intent, your amygdala would see the difference and sound the alarm bells.

3. Sort for Group Membership: Is it "Me" or "We"?

The next phase of our belonging biology, still happening in an instantaneous cascade, is sorting for members of our same group or tribe. We are tribal beings and our bodies naturally scan for whether we are part of a "we" with others. Scientists call this an in-group/out-group assessment or social categorization, because we are trying to determine what relationship we have to the other person. If we are part of the same tribe, we likely relax a little further.

The brain structure that plays a key role in this process is the medial prefrontal cortex (MPFC) and it helps us determined whether, in any interaction, we are there as an individual self (that is, it's me) or part of a collective self (as in, we're a "we"). This part of brain developed for a time when we lived in small tribes on the plains and likely only encountered a few other tribes in our lifetimes. Human identity was tightly enmeshed with the hundred or so other individuals with whom we lived with, sharing duties to provide food, shelter, and protection.

But now we are all part of several collectives or tribes over the course of our lifetimes. Here are some that come to mind:

- Biological family (we're the Johnsons or Patels).
- Neighborhood (we're Montavillans or Brooklynites)
- Community/city (we're Parisians or Houstonians)
- School (we're Falcons or Bruins)
- Workplace (we're Googlers or Peetniks)
- Occupation (we're engineers or writers)
- State/region (we're Californians or Alabamans)
- Country/nation (we're Canadians or Pakistanis)
- Race and ethnicity (we're African American or Asian Venezuelan)

- Religion/spirituality (we're Catholics or Buddhists or agnostic)
- Political affiliation (we're Democrats or Republicans, Labour or Conservative)
- Hobbies/interests (we're cyclists or knitters or flamenco dancers)
- Organizations (we're Federalists or World Wildlife Funders)
- Beliefs/ideologies (we're missionaries or environmentalists)
- Pet owners (we're dog people or cat people)

If you want to see a sample of our tribes, just look at the bumper stickers on cars around you on your next drive. Many people display one or two that are meaningful to them; some go all out.

We now have many places we "belong," and we often juggle memberships in many groups simultaneously. In fact, neuroscientists have found that our social categorization is rather flexible and fluid. We can and do often shift our sense of membership, one minute feeling connected to our neighbors, the next feeling a kinship with the residents of our state, and just moments later feeling a strong connection to our nationality. We easily move up and down this continuum of scale, according to doctors Mina Cikara and Jay Van Bavel: "Social identities become more inclusive as the context makes more abstract identities salient (for example, shifting from local to national to global identities), leading to the inclusion of others who would otherwise be deemed as distinct from the self." We see this all the time with natural disasters. People who normally avoid or judge each other come together and help complete strangers.

This social categorization is so fluid that scientists can test aspects of it by simply putting subjects in arbitrary groups. For example, one study took subjects of different races (one social category with which people have a lifelong relationship), and sorted them into a red team and a blue team (a new social category). This simple new social categorization of being part of a group overrode race, even on a neurological level.

Several studies have tested this with consistent results. Once we see ourselves as part of a "we," our biology shifts. We become an "us" that exists in relation to a "them." Neurologically, we respond differently to members we perceive as part of our group. A series of studies have shown that an unconscious bias gets activated. We evaluate the performance of our group more favorably, we remember events and "facts" in a way that elevates them (for example, our team was faster and stronger in our minds than neutral observers saw), and we are more likely to give them rewards. This bias for our group is part of how we bond and belong.

Fortunately, it seems to be one-sided. Our brains can hold an "us *and* them" perspective. But it does mean that we need to be aware of this effect and perhaps take people's evaluations and memories of how awesome their group is with a grain of salt. This grain of salt also applies to our own evaluations and memories as well.

Unconscious bias often plays out during the hiring process when interviewers who believe they are being objective feel more connected to applicants who are similar to themselves. The brain takes a shortcut, miscoding the familiar as comfortable, and this invisibly influences how we view and evaluate others. Unconscious bias has also been shown to affect what we remember and report about an incident, which can have important implications for the fairness of the judicial process. Everyone has unconscious bias, as it's part of our neurological wiring, but we can learn to watch for its effects and take counter measures to reduce its influence.

This "me or we" or "us and them" sort is biologically powerful. It fuels much of our daily life as we find ways to align and affiliate with our group because it gives us that sense of belonging, something we hunger for. Bumper stickers, fashions and fads (think lapel pins, tote bags, clothing, jewelry, hairstyles, and tattoos), and so on become a way we easily display our membership in something meaningful to us as well as identify our tribe members. These cues have also have become how we identify the "others." A rainbow flag or a headscarf can simultaneously be a beacon for people who share a life experience or set of values, or it can be a magnet for hatred and harm. The difference comes from whether we have moved to a view of "us *versus* them."

4. Assess for Us Versus Them

Finally, our brain takes one last step, which is to determine if we have an "us *versus* them" relationship with the out-group. Out-groups can range from neutral to nefarious and our brain sorts to see if we have an active and hostile relationship with them. This is an important distinction because it deeply impacts our biology. In us-versus-them perception, we see more positive things for the "us," our in-group.

We extend empathy to them, for example, and if they do something negative we forgive them. When they succeed, we take pleasure, which activates the reward centers of our brain. We are also more likely to engage in acts of altruism for our "us" people, like helping or sending donations.

Simultaneously, this orientation activates negative things for the "them" group, who are seen as a threatening enemy. The reward part of our brain still lights up, but now it happens for the failures of others, giving us a sense of pleasure when they lose. It activates judgment, making it easier to find fault. And it activates hostility and derogation, making it easy to not see rivals as equals, or even human, thus justifying aggression against them.

Even further, while empathy is automatically wired for in-group affiliations, it's not only decreased but actually missing for out-groups, making it harder to perceive others' sadness and physical pain. We instead use apathy, or worse, antipathy.

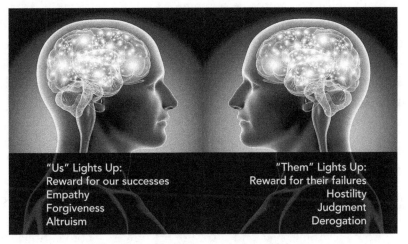

How "us vs. them" impacts attitudes and behavior

The purpose of this response is to aid us in winning the perceived tribal war. We become more attached to our group and act in ways that help us as a group, and we become more hostile to the other group, making it easier to harm them should it come to that.

Obviously, these behaviors offer biological benefits if you live in a true war zone and resources are scarce. Your very survival may depend on it. You may need to snatch food out of the hands of another to feed your own children. You may need to attack someone who is coming for your family.

To override our inherent human nature to care for one another and to feel each other's pain, we have to make them less than us. We have to strip away their humanity. In his book, *Less Than Human: Why We Demean, Enslave, and Exterminate Others,* David Smith explains that we have deep biological inhibitions that prevent us from physically and psychologically harming others. Dehumanization is how we override that.

Seeing someone as the enemy and a threat to your survival is the beginning of the dehumanization process. In *Braving the Wilderness,* Dr. Brené Brown writes, "Dehumanizing others is the process by which we become accepting of violations against human nature, the human spirit, and, for many of us, violations against the central tenets of our faith."

Dr. Michelle Maiese says this process begins by creating an image of the enemy where they are framed as dangerous, inferior, and even evil. Once this is in place, it's easy for people to believe that, for their own survival, the other must be defeated. There is no "and"—it's an "or" with only one acceptable outcome.

In some conflicts, there truly may be only so much food, or the other group will kill you if you don't kill them first. But in many conflicts this dehumanization process is intentionally activated by leaders who hope to further their own status or group. They begin a methodical and systematic framing that forces a wedge between friends and neighbors until they were willing to turn on each other, harm, and even kill.

Sadly, this is not a thing of the past nor is it contained to geographic wars. Current headlines are filled with stories about leaders who cast groups of people as threatening to our jobs, our way of life, our happiness, and our safety, even in the absence of evidence. These leaders know how to push the tribal buttons in people's brains to influence how they think, feel, and act. With the power of conventional and social media, this process can unfold even more quickly and powerfully than in the past.

So how does this play out with teams in our workplaces? Many leaders believe that creating a highly competitive environment brings out the best in people. So they pit teams and groups against each other in a real fight for resources and recognition, triggering our us-versus-them biology. While this may drive a short-term burst in productivity or innovation, it actually creates much longer term and harmful negative consequences.

Microsoft is an example of this. For years, senior leaders pitted groups against each other in a tough competition for projects and resources. They also adopted a performance review system that used forced rankings where only so many employees could receive high marks. This led to a culture of fear and competition that caused employees to sabotage each other's work and managers to bargain and trade votes in the annual group review process. In a now famous *Vanity Fair* article titled "Microsoft's Lost Decade," author Kurt Eichenwald writes, "The story of Microsoft's lost decade could serve as a business-school case study on the pitfalls of success. Staffers were rewarded not just for doing well but for making sure that their colleagues failed. As a result, the company was consumed by an endless series of internal knife fights. Potential market-busting businesses—such as ebook and smartphone technology—were killed, derailed, or delayed amid bickering and power plays." While Microsoft ditched the stack rankings in 2013, many say that Microsoft has yet to fully recover, despite new CEO Satya Nadella's efforts to build a growth mindset culture.

Certainly, a little mild rivalry between teams can be motivating and even productive. But if the leaders set people up to drive a strong us-versus-them mentality, they will ultimately harm the effectiveness of their organization because the brain does not easily override the foe/them categorization. Once someone is placed in the foe/them category, people engage from a place of judgment and antipathy—the antithesis of psychological safety. It will take a lot of extra and intentional work to train their brains to respond differently.

In today's workplaces, where reorganizations are frequent and work groups must be agile and adaptive, having your employees trust each other less and less will only undermine your organization's success. Each shuffle brings the likelihood that people will be placed on the same side as a former rival. But just because a shift is made on paper, it doesn't mean they shift biologically. Needless to say, this will undermine communication and trust, which will severely damage productivity, engagement, and innovation.

Your priority should be to move people to at least a place of "us *and* them" but ideally you want to activate a feeling of belonging and the "sense of we."

Case Study: Digital Marketing Agency
Org Size: Small

"As a venture-backed company that started as a software company with professional support we got advice that the company would be best positioned as a digital marketing agency with supporting software. This required a restructure of the company to align with this new vision. Team leads were moved into new positions as account directors where they had roles that were unfamiliar to them, and people that once reported to them were promoted to lead their old teams, and were now peers.

Because of the nature of the team split, there was an 'us versus them' mentality. The account directors had objectives that overlapped with the client delivery department, which caused conflict between the teams on how client demands would be executed. The account director felt threatened and pointed fingers at the client delivery group.

To build morale, the client delivery group did team-building workshops, which helped us become more aligned and better able to deal with the stress of this high-pressure environment. These workshops helped us stay motivated, build trust, and improve communication. As a result, we consistently accomplished the clients' goals and earned high net promoter scores (NPS).

However, the company remained siloed so it felt like an uphill battle. We didn't feel like we had the support of our VPs as they were fighting bigger power struggles at the executive level. A lot of the high-performing team members left for greener pastures. I eventually left after experiencing ongoing burnout in this volatile work environment."

15. Impact of Age and Media

It is interesting to note that our ability to sort for "me and we" shifts from childhood to adulthood. Dr. Joao Moreira and other researchers at the University of North Carolina's Department of Psychology and Neuroscience found that, as children, we only scan for potential threat or danger. So, if someone doesn't display those markers, they are automatically part of the child's in-group. This is why kids so quickly can say, "You're my friend" after meeting someone for a few seconds. Essentially, anyone nonthreatening is now part of our "we."

In other words, we are truly born wired to connect with others. Seeing people as different or bad comes from socialization; the way children are shaped by parents, teachers, and the media. We are taught who we include in our tribe and perhaps more importantly, who we don't. For example, a child's brain doesn't really "see" race for the first five or six years. So, anyone can be a friend and only threatening people are foes. While children begin to notice skin tone differences around first grade—parents of every background have had to deal with the innocent but sometimes awkward questions—children will assign it the meaning that the adults in their life tell them to.

In a series of studies by Dr. Van Bavel at New York University's Center for Neural Science, he found that while the growing brain can "see" race, it doesn't automatically perceive it as a sign of out-group status. In one study, titled "Is Race Erased? Decoding Race from Patterns of Neural Activity When Skin Color Is Not Diagnostic of Group Boundaries," Van Bavel's group assigned people of different ethnicities to a group, instantly creating their sense of being part of a group. While seeing people of difference races activated the brain's visual cortex more than for same-race members, this does not seem to translate to emotions or behaviors.

The researchers concluded, "Returning to Martin Luther King Jr., although the words 'perceived' and 'judged' are often used interchangeably, it is notable that he dreamt that his children would not be 'judged' by the color of their skin. Perhaps King recognized that 'seeing' race is not inherently problematic for race relations. It is what the mind subsequently does with this information that matters."

Parents and teachers play a significant role in our views too. I have a distinct memory from when I was seven years old of my grandmother locking the car door whenever we crossed over this one street, which demarcated the white neighborhood we lived in from the areas where people looked different. She never said the words, but I got the message loud and clear. And that message was reinforced by the lack of diversity in our friends and neighbors and then exacerbated by what I saw on TV shows and movies.

This is why media matters so much, especially in children's developmental years. If our brains are presented with many images of certain groups of people posing as threats (for example, shown as criminals or terrorists), our brain almost treats those images as memories.

Scientists have long known the power of the media. Several researchers studied the impact on people and our society during the time television was invented and becoming a regular component of American homes. Studies by doctors George Gerbner and Larry Gross have consistently showed that exposure to crime shows (such as *Law and Order*, *CSI*, and *Bones* today and *Adam-12*, *Kojak*, and *Columbo* back then) increases viewers' fear that they will become a victim of a crime. Several similar studies led to the creation of the Mean and Scary World Syndrome, which essentially states that viewers of violent media are significantly more likely to overrate the amount of crime that actually happens, believing that there are murders, rapists, and pedophiles everywhere.

These studies are familiar to me as I studied them while earning my master's degree in communication and mass media. The overwhelming number of studies is conclusive: media alters our beliefs and behaviors because our brain sees the images as real. In other words, these are not just made-up scenes on a screen but rather they are perceived as the real actions of people who live near our tribe. Here are some findings from studies that might surprise you:

- By age 12, the average American child will have watched 8,000 murders on television. By age 18, that number will grow to 40,000 murders and 200,000 other acts of violence (assault, battery, rape, etc.).

- Longitudinal studies have shown that violent programming watched as children is related to aggression at school as well as more criminal behavior as adults, and higher levels of aggression against their spouses and children.

- In 2008, the then-chairman of the Federal Communications Commission (FCC), Reed Hundt stated, "There is no longer any serious debate about whether violence in the media is a legitimate problem. Science and commonsense judgments of parents agree. As stated in a year-long effort, funded by the cable-TV industry. . .'there are substantial risks of harmful effects from viewing violence throughout the television environment.'"

- When television viewing becomes common in a society, murder rates skyrocket (a study that has been replicated in many countries).

Violence is not the only message we are getting from our televisions. It also tells our brains what to perceive about our neighbors. The average American adult spends one-third of their free time watching television. Consider what takeaways we get from these statistics:

- Women represent less than one-third of all characters, even though they are half of the population.

- Lower-income people, who make up about 13 percent of the population, are only represented by 1.3 percent of characters in prime-time shows.

- For every white male victim, there are 17 white female victims and 22 minority female victims.

- "Bad guys" are overwhelmingly represented as male, poor, young, and of color or foreign.

- Heavy television viewers view the world to be much more dangerous than do light viewers, and tend to favor and support increased justice measures like capital punishments, building more prisons, etc.

And that's just television shows. Video games and apps also expose us to violence but now instead of being an observing bystander, we can be in the action, pulling a real trigger to shoot and kill others. Each instance adds more information to our brains that see it all as real.

So what does it mean when a brain categorizes entire segments of society as "foes" or "thems"? It becomes more fearful and anxious about our safety and we become less trusting of others, but we don't always know why on a conscious level.

Unconscious Bias

This is where unconscious bias comes from: early images and messages that impact our neurobiology and our 200-millisecond response to certain groups. We all have unconscious bias, and how our brain categorizes people reflects the socialization we received in whatever country and community we were raised in. Unconscious bias impacts us more than we realize, ranging from a mild sensation of unease or distrust to a strong reaction of fear and loathing. It colors how we perceive another's intentions, words, and body language. It impacts what we are looking for and ultimately what we find.

If you grew up being fed a constant diet of African Americans as criminals, then every behavior is suspect—driving a nice car, walking through a store, and wearing a hoodie. And if the stereotype is scary, the reptilian/survival brain will of course prepare for an imminent danger, setting off our fight-flight-freeze response. The amygdala floods the body with chemicals that fuel strength and reactivity while shutting down logical thinking and self-awareness. To the amygdala, every shadow is a potential gun, and every movement is an attack. Once this response is activated, we lose our thinking brain and self-awareness that might help us overcome this response under calmer circumstances.

While we have come a long way as a society, it was only a few years ago that our society was filled with *overt* and enforced messages about the following negative stereotypes:

- Women as weak/emotional
- African Americans as criminals
- Latinos as lazy
- Jews as miserly
- Gay/lesbian/transgender people as depraved
- Asians as inscrutable
- Pacific Islanders as shifty
- Hippies as dirty
- Millennials as too fragile

These views were widely held, and many would argue still are although perhaps more covertly. They have been endlessly amplified and replicated in our TV shows, textbooks, policies, and laws. While many people have realized that these stereotypes are erroneous, it takes time and intentional effort to unlearn and dismantle them, both on an individual level as well as in our society. And these elements shape us more dramatically than we might imagine and impact how we see others, even on a neurological level.

Stereotypes work in insidious ways. Just being on the receiving end of a stereotype can harm people's sense of self. Researchers have found that people can start to believe the stereotypes about their group, even when they know they are not true, an effect called internalized oppression. When this happens, stereotyped people start to unconsciously incorporate the myths and misinformation that society communicates to them into their self-image. For example, women might internalize the stereotype that they are not good at math or science, impacting the subjects they study in college as well as careers they pursue. Are we really surprised then that there is a shortage of women in the science and computing fields?

Similarly, people of color might internalize the myth that they are supposed to be intellectually inferior. And lower-income people might believe that they are worth less than wealthy people, so they don't pursue opportunities such as a college education and higher paying careers. This in turn creates a self-perpetuating cycle that gets passed down through the generations, widening the gap between groups.

Stereotypes also affect people's capabilities and performance. Called the "stereotype threat," several studies have shown that being viewed through negative stereotypes can trigger the survival/reptilian brain, which of course turns off the thinking, neocortex brain and temporarily reducing our intelligence. This can impede people from performing at even an average level, much less at their best.

Several studies have proven this effect for all kinds of groups. One study found that when African American students were asked to identify their race when taking a standardized test, they consistently performed lower than other African American students who were not asked to do so. In another study, women were asked to take a notoriously difficult math ability test. Participants were randomly assigned to one of three groups, labeled as women, residents of the Northeast, or students at an elite private college. The third group (elite college) consistently performed the best on the exam, even though all the labels were true of all the women.

Stereotypes inevitably impact the beliefs, values, and actions of others, and the prejudice can cause them to deny people access to opportunities. For example, not interviewing female applicants for engineering jobs or not renting a home to a family of color.

In 2018, women still make 20 percent less than what men make for the same job. This translates to 44 extra days of work for a woman to earn what a man does. Iceland reported a gap of 18 percent, calculating that women were essentially working for free after 2:38 p.m. each day. Women continue to be overrepresented in the lower-paying occupations. In 2017, the *Fortune* 500 list contains only 32 female CEOs, which is a paltry 6.4 percent even though 49.6 percent of the world's population is female. It's the first year a Latina was named CEO, one of two women of color. Ironically, the headline in *Fortune* magazine read "The 2017 Fortune 500 Includes Record Number of Women CEOs." Globally, only 13 countries are led by women, which again is the highest number ever. The news about sexual predators like Harvey Weinstein, Matt Lauer, Roy Moore, and Bill O'Reilly demonstrate the additional threats women often endure at work.

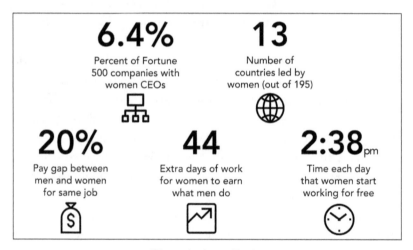

Women in the world today

Currently and historically, African Americans are extremely overrepresented in the US prison systems, a reflection of racial profiling and biased laws and sentencing. While African Americans are 13 percent of the US population, they comprise 38 percent of the state prison system, meaning that they are incarcerated at an average of 5.1 times the rate of whites (in some states it's as high as 10:1).

Lesbian, gay, bisexual, transgender (LGBT) people are often the victims of harassment, discrimination, and violence (including torture and murder) around the world. According to Amnesty International, 76 countries still criminalize same-sex relationships. Human Rights

Watch tracks, documents, and exposes issues impacting several groups including LGBT people. They have highlighted harmful practices from a wide range of countries including conversion therapy in China, attacks on LGBT activists in Moscow, and forced sterilization in Japan. In 2016, excluding victims at the Pulse nightclub in Florida, 28 LGBT people were killed, a 17 percent increase from the previous year. When LGBT-identified Pulse victims are included (the intended targets), the murder rate rose 217 percent in 2016.

Today, you can still see these old stereotypes at play preventing the members of marginalized groups from achieving full equality in society. While the gaps have closed a little in the past few years, we are still a long way from equality. And today, we have the additional negative stereotypes of Muslims as terrorists and Middle-Eastern immigrants as draining resources and taking all of "our" jobs.

In just the first half of 2017, hate crimes against Muslims increased 91 percent in the United States. Islamophobic acts included physical violence, harassment, and property damage. Victims were most likely to be targeted in their homes followed by on the road or street. In addition, acts of bias against Muslims rose by 24 percent compared with the same period in 2016.

While a small percentage of the population knowingly believes stereotypes and intentionally uses them to guide actions (supremacy and extremist groups, for example), the majority happens through unconscious bias, with some of us acting in ways we are not even conscious of.

Counterbalancing Stereotypes

This is why unconscious bias and inclusion programs are so important in our schools and workplaces. It can help us become aware of these invisible forces and make different choices.

For example, the stereotype threat can be counterbalanced through intentional actions. Researchers at New York University helped marginalized middle school students raise both their test scores and admission rates to magnet high schools by helping them understand, through a series of discussions, that their abilities were determined by what they could do and not their gender or race.

I find Stanford University Dr. Geoffrey Cohen's research on this topic particularly compelling. In one study, subjects were asked to spend 15 minutes writing about something that was important to them and why. This brief exercise boosted their confidence, acting like a "mental vaccine" against the stereotype threat.

In another study, Dr. Cohen worked with African American college students, who often worry about not being accepted by their peers due to their race. Dr. Cohen did a one-hour session with the students during their first term, focusing on the studies and statistics that show these are common worries for all students, and that they disappear with time. In other words, he intentionally counterbalanced the effect of the stereotype threat. The results were astounding. At graduation, the achievement gap between the African American students and their white peers was halved. Additionally, the students were physically healthier and emotionally happier than the control group of African American students.

Case Study: Manufacturing Firm
Org Size: Small

"In my organization there are three separate groups in Strategic Sourcing and Partnerships. Each group is responsible for heading up an employee engagement/involvement team and work on projects that affect your group. There can be a range of projects from creating and implementing a new process to building new tools, websites, etc.

I'm on the supply chain group and we have been working together on a variety of projects over the last couple years. There are six of us on the team and we meet in person each week. We all bring different views, backgrounds and levels of experience to the table as well as skills, strengths and weaknesses.

The biggest thing we have managed to accomplish is to create a really safe environment. We are comfortable asking questions and sharing ideas or concerns with each other. The input from each team member helps us see things from a different point of view and examine possible outcomes we had not thought of. This has also created a fun work dynamic, where we share best practices and enjoy camaraderie with bantering and joking.

The results of the team include successful projects and the pride the team has around what we have accomplished. I think our respect for each other and the differences we bring is the most positive contributor to this team's success and how well we work together."

Scientific American magazine featured Dr. Cohen's work in an article titled "Armored Against Prejudice." In it, author Ed Yong details several key studies that prove again and again that the stereotype threat is real, pervasive, and impacting the success of large communities of people—but again concludes that these harmful effects can be intentionally counterbalanced. This is where our potential lives: in the fact that when we are told we are capable of more, we perform better. And when we are told that effort and improvement matters, we improve.

Most importantly, I think, is that the research shows us that as a species we ultimately orient to "others" the way our leaders tell us to. Leaders—parents, executives, teachers, media personalities, elected officials, and so on—are incredibly powerful, and they can either use their positions to unite or divide. When leaders help us see each other as citizens of the same country, neighbors in the same community, and members of the same team, our brains reconfigure those people to be our in-group. This can override old and erroneous messages by drawing new lines. Stating "we are a we," can soothe our reptilian brain so we settle down and can perform at our best.

The Benefits of Diversity

Leaders who value diversity reap all kinds of benefits for their organization. Several different studies have explored the impact diversity has on groups. Here are some key findings:

- Diverse groups are more innovative (they outperform homogeneous groups on creative problem solving)
- Diverse groups make fewer errors (they focus on facts better and identify potential problems more than homogeneous groups)
- Diverse groups are better able to handle and resolve conflict

When leaders value and support diversity across their organization, all of the above benefits multiply, making diverse organizations more successful on several levels. Their financial returns are as much as 35 percent above their industry average. They experience both higher return on equity and income growth compared to their less diverse counterparts. Diversity also increases employee engagement and reduces turnover, both of which can generate huge financial benefits. It's no wonder that the *New York Times* recently ran an article titled "150 Executives Commit to Fostering Diversity and Inclusion" featuring companies like Procter & Gamble, New York Life, Accenture, and Deloitte.

It's important to remember that diversity is not just about race and gender. Diversity includes age, ethnicity, spirituality, sexual orientation, political views, work styles, and more. In fact, Millennials (who now make up 53.5 percent of the workforce) view diversity much more broadly than their Gen X and Boomer colleagues, considering things like the unique viewpoints and experiences that can be brought to the team or organization. They are 22 percent more likely to focus on bringing together diverse people to gain the value that comes from learning from and working with others. Millennials also care deeply about inclusion, which plays a vital role in bringing out the best in diverse groups. We'll learn why in section IV.

Your Learning Journey

Let's explore the brain science of safety and belonging.
- Over your professional life, have you seen or experienced workplace bullying, harassment, or violence? What impact did it have on you and the others involved?
- Have you ever experienced a leader framing things as "us versus them" at work? What did they say or do to convey that? How did it impact your experience?
- Knowing that media has shaped our perceptions and beliefs, what are some stereotypes you see people believing about others?
- Have you been part of diverse teams? How did different perspectives or experiences impact the group? Did you have ways of working through the inevitable but healthy conflict?

THE BRAIN SCIENCE OF INCLUSION & TRUST

"If you are not actively working to make your team members feel part of an inclusive, supportive group, then there are a number of ways (many subtle and unintentional) that you may be creating an environment of social exclusion and its resulting negative consequences."

Dr. Christine Cox, New York University
Langone Medical Center

16. Inclusion and Exclusion

We are experiencing an important and much-needed shift in our understanding of what brings out the best in people, thanks to new findings in neuroscience. Our understanding of how people develop thoughts and beliefs about others and how these shape their attitudes and actions is becoming more clear. This is why many companies now offer learning programs on unconscious bias and inclusion.

Biologically, we are wired to assess where we stand in our group: While a young child's brain only sorts for friend or foe, the adolescent brain develops more nuanced capabilities. One study found that as we enter adolescence our brain shifts to prioritize the in-group; this neurological response starts around age ten and launches the beginning of self-consciousness. It is also part of our drive to survive and belong—our body essentially prepares us to leave the nest of our family so we're able to successfully live in our larger community. This is why peer influence becomes so prevalent for tweens and teens. "Peer pressure" is not just a catch phrase; it's the result of our brains sorting for what our in-group thinks, so we can find our place.

From the perspective of our tribal brain, if we are outcast from the group we are likely to perish. Being able to scan for the peer group's values and preferences gives us tools to navigate our communities and increase our chances of being accepted by the group. Our brain has the ability to quickly assess our social status in a group as well as our position in our friendship network. Researchers at Northwestern University found that one of the regions involved, the inferior parietal lobe, is the same part of the brain that tracks numbers and scalar magnitudes. Essentially, the brain keeps a running tally of where we stand in our ranking in the group.

Dr. Rita Tavares, from the Schiller Laboratory of Affective Neurosciences at the Icahn School of Medicine at Mount Sinai, has found that the entorhinal cortex within the hippocampus plays a vital role in how we map our social networks. The entorhinal cortex works as our internal GPS, helping us to build mental maps of physical and social spaces, like our workplaces and neighborhoods. It also creates mental maps of our social networks, in particular noting power and affinity. Our ability to succeed socially depends on these maps helping us navigate complex relationships and power dynamics.

As we enter new social spaces, like jobs or neighborhoods, our brain scans for information and is actually able to map relationships based on power (including hierarchy, dominance, competence) as well as affinity (including trustworthiness, love, intimacy). Functional neuro-imaging scanners (fMRI) show that navigating new social settings activates the hippocampus, proof that the mapping function is taking place.

Our brain is highly tuned to signs that we are being marginalized, or pushed out to the edges rather than being in the middle where we are safest. The amygdala, which is part of the survival/reptilian brain, is the brain structure most active and sensitive to social status. Researchers at John Hopkins and Arizona State Universities have measured increased activity in the amygdala and increased levels of cortisol, the stress hormone, in the bloodstream in relation to where a subject was placed in their friendship network. Dr. Nathan DeWall, a psychologist at the University of Kentucky describes it this way, "Humans have a fundamental need to belong. Just as we have needs for food and water, we also have needs for positive and lasting relationships. This need is deeply rooted in our evolutionary history."

Exclusion Causes Pain

One of the shocking discoveries I made while researching this book was that exclusion lights up the *same* regions of the brain as *physical pain*. Think about that.

Being excluded registers as pain, as if you've been slapped in the face or worse. Perhaps it's because emotional injury is just as threatening to our survival as a physical injury.

And this isn't just one random study but a consistent finding by researchers at Harvard, Purdue, Duke, and UCLA, to name a few. As Dr. Kipling Williams, a psychologist at Purdue University states, "Being excluded is painful because it threatens fundamental human needs, such as belonging and self-esteem. Again and again research has found that strong, harmful reactions are possible even when ostracized by a stranger for a short amount of time." For example, a study he conducted with Dr. Naomi Eisenberg at UCLA found that the same parts of the brain activate for social rejection as do for physical pain (the insula and the dorsal anterior cingulate). Using fMRI machines, the researchers created an experience of mild exclusion by having subjects play an online game of catch, called cyberball, with two other players. Then the two players excluded the subject and played without him or her. The pain center of the excluded person lit up, creating a new understanding of why exclusion is so uncomfortable for us all.

In a similar study at the University of Michigan, Dr. Ethan Kross gathered subjects who had a romantic partner break things off. He asked them to look at photos of their exes and again found that the same regions lit up as for physical pain.

Another study explored whether this pain reaction could be lessened or mitigated. Subjects were offered money when they were rejected, but not when they were accepted. But the compensation did nothing to change the pain reaction. Dr. Williams also tried his cyber-ball experiment again, this time testing to see what happened when subjects were rejected by someone they did not like. He used African American students and told them that the people rejecting them were members of the Ku Klux Klan. But even knowing that information did not change the pain reaction in the brain. "No matter how hard you push it, people are hurt by ostracism," he states.

Researchers have also explored whether social pain can be treated medically, in the same way as physical pain. Pain medications like opioids work in the brain, not by making the pain of a broken arm go away, but by disconnecting the pain receptors in our brain so we don't feel it. When the drug wears off, the sensation of pain flows again. Over-the-counter medications, like Advil, do the same thing on a smaller scale.

DeWall and Eisenberger partnered to explore the effect of pain medications on social pain by giving subjects an over-the-counter pain medication, acetaminophen, and then measuring their reaction to exclusion on the fMRI. Sure enough, compared to the group with a placebo those who had taken the pain medication had less activity in the pain regions of their brain when they were being rejected.

I suspect that one of the reasons we are experiencing this tragic opioid epidemic in the US is that people go on pain meds for legitimate physical injuries, but find that they also get a respite from their social pain. Once they are physically healed, they can't quite face the reality of their social pain. And our society does not yet do a good job at helping people talk about that and offer ways to heal from it. In fact, we further reject them and shame them for their drug abuse problems.

17. Stages of Rejection

Dr. Williams has done several further studies with Dr. Steve Nida to explore the aftereffects of exclusion. They have found three stages of exclusion or ostracism:

1. Initial act of being ignored
2. Coping
3. Resignation

During the initial act of being ignored, the brain registers the experience as a type of pain. Williams has studied over 5,000 people and has found that even two to three minutes of exclusion creates lingering negative feelings.

Next, in the coping stage they found people tend to have one of two responses to exclusion. Some people try harder to be included, engaging in behaviors designed to help them get re-integrated into the group, such as conforming, complying, and cooperating. "They will pay more attention to social cues and try to be more likable," Williams says. Picture the familiar scene of a person's raised hand enthusiastically saying, "Pick me! Pick me!"

But when people feel that there is little hope of re-inclusion, they are likely to seek inclusion elsewhere, essentially rejecting the group that rejected them. Researchers found that the less control people had in their lives, the more likely they were to lash out and be less helpful. Now picture that same hand raised, but with a different kind of gesture as they say, "Screw you!"

1. Initial act of being ignored   2. Coping   3. Resignation

The three stages of rejection

The third stage is resignation, which happens when exclusion or ostracism occurs over a long time—like at school or work where people have to return every day to an environment where they feel they do not belong.

Another study by DeWall found that people who were suffering from long-term exclusion were less able to perform on difficult tasks, had poor impulse control, poorer sleep quality, and immune systems that did not function as well as their peers who were included. People in this stage experience sadness, anxiety, depression, helplessness, along with feelings of unworthiness. It's no surprise that substance abuse and suicide are common responses. Alcohol and drug abuse, and other addictions, are ways people try to self-medicate to relieve the immediate pain; however, this short-term relief tends to lead to a downward spiral of guilt, shame, and further rejection. As Williams put it, "Long-term ostracism seems to be very devastating. People finally give up."

On the other hand, some sufferers take a different route, becoming increasingly angry. They not only become less helpful, they may become openly hostile and even aggressive. "When a person feels ostracized they feel out of control, and aggressive behavior is one way to restore that control," he says. Aggression at work can take all kinds of forms including criticism, contempt, sarcasm, teasing, and shaming, not to mention physical and emotional intimidation, bullying, harassment, and abuse. I'm struck by how similar this sounds to Gallup's definition of an actively disengaged person at work, "Actively disengaged employees aren't just unhappy at work; they're busy acting out their unhappiness. Every day, these workers undermine what their engaged coworkers accomplish." It can also lead to misusing resources and benefits, like stealing office supplies and misrepresenting vacation hours. No wonder Gallup estimates that disengaged employees cost companies 34 percent of their annual salaries.

So, colleagues who are acting out not only further their own sense of rejection, they may also sow the seeds of exclusion and disengagement in others. A study by Drs. Christine Porath and Christine Pearson, titled *The Cost of Bad Behavior*, found that rude or uncivil behavior on the part of one employee negatively impacts their colleagues in a multitude of ways. Consider these results:

- 80 percent lost work time worrying about the incident
- 78 percent said their commitment to the organization declined

- 66 percent felt their performance declined
- 63 percent lost time avoiding the offender
- 48 percent intentionally decreased their work effort
- 47 percent intentionally decreased time at work
- 38 percent intentionally decreased work quality
- 12 percent left the organization

This is why employee engagement surveys matter, because they can give you valuable data about the health of teams and departments and identify where a domino effect might be in play or about to start as the contagion effect of mirror neurons kick in.

Case Study: Middle School
Org Size: Small

"The goal was to improve student learning by bringing all the teachers in one room to collaborate on various aspects of teaching the subject matter. It was believed that working together, the teachers could use data to create meaningful lessons along with common assessments. We also wanted to insure that an A in one teachers class would be an A in another teacher's class. We were given literature to read about these Professional Learning Communities (PLCs,) but never really were told how to do them. We were pretty much on our own with no real guidance—the only requirement was that we meet once a week for at least half an hour.

Our team (seventh grade history) consisted of four teachers. I had 12 years of experience and was appointed the lead as my other two teammates had both been teaching less than one year. The fourth teacher had been teaching for 12 years but not in a middle school setting. I believe that some of our team dysfunction was that we were making a lot up as we went along and half of the group didn't have much experience. Myself and one of the new teachers ('Jane') both had strong opinions, which did not align and we expressed disagreement. But the other two members stayed quiet. We didn't try to listen to each other. As the frustration grew so did the tension in the room. It was not a pleasant experience for all.

Then the two new teachers became good friends and they started resisting anything I suggested. It felt like my experience meant nothing or that I was an 'old' teacher so what I knew was no good. Not wanting to rock the boat, I gave in and went along with Jane's ideas. Little did I know that Jane was telling other people that I was not being a team player and causing tension. This unfortunately became a repeating pattern, I would suggest something in our meetings and Jane would say it was wrong and we couldn't do it. I then would hear from others that I was once again the source of tension. As the team leader I tried to see if I could maybe work to get things back on track with where they had to be. I would ask if everything was okay with how things were going and if they had any issues they wanted to discuss, but Jane would say nothing. Jane started emailing out meeting agendas to the group, which had been my responsibility. I just gave up trying to be the team lead and handed it off to Jane.

After that, I was going through the motions and I just took the path of least resistance. Why should I try if my opinions are not valued and she's going to be rude to me? It was difficult to look at her with all that I knew she was saying to others about me. I started to feel like crap about going to the meetings. I would get physically sick. Even now, writing about this situation that occurred six years ago makes me sick to my stomach. This all happened years ago but the hurt still lingers, that's how much of a struggle it was."

Williams found that people who respond to long-term exclusion with aggression can also pose a greater threat to their communities, sometimes by escalating into violence. Duke University neuroscientist Dr. Mark Leary analyzed fifteen cases of school shooters and found that thirteen of them (86 percent) suffered from ongoing social rejection.

The 2017 mass shooting of concert goers in Las Vegas, Nevada, and church members in Sutherland Spring, Texas, as well as the 2018 school shooting at Douglas high school in Parkland, Florida were all committed by men who had a history of social difficulties, perhaps stemming from mental illness.

The National Safety Council urges that every organization be prepared for workplace violence and the potential of active shooters. They also recommend training for employees on what to do if workplace violence erupts and to look out for these warning signs:

- Excessive use of alcohol or drugs
- Unexplained absenteeism, change in behavior, or decline in job performance
- Depression, withdrawal, or suicidal comments
- Resistance to changes at work or persistent complaining about unfair treatment
- Violation of company policies
- Emotional responses to criticism, mood swings
- Paranoia

Sound familiar? These are the same symptoms of people suffering from long-term exclusion.

Another way that chronic exclusion can impact us all is that extremist groups intentionally prey on the ostracized and rejected. Williams states, "These group provide members with a sense of belonging, self-worth, and control, but they can fuel narrowness, radicalism, and intolerance, and perhaps a propensity toward hostility and violence toward others." These groups offer immediate relief, often framing the rejecters as the source of the problem and encouraging members to aim their energy at getting even. Dr. Arie Kruglanski, at the University of Maryland who studies violent extremism, says, "There are strong correlations between humiliation and the search for an extremist ideology."

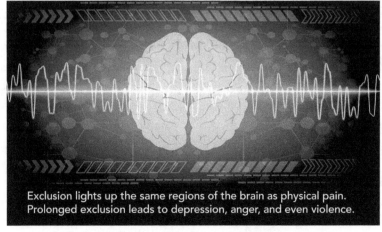

Exclusion lights up the same regions of the brain as physical pain. Prolonged exclusion leads to depression, anger, and even violence.

The long-term effects of exclusion harm individuals and communities

Take for example the man who drove a truck down a bike lane in New York City, killing and injuring several cyclists and pedestrians. He stated that he "felt good" about what he had done and asked if he could hang the terrorist group ISIS's flag in his hospital room.

Naturally concerned, researchers wondered what if anything might mitigate the tendency for excluded people to choose aggression. Dr. DeWall did a couple of experiments where subjects experienced exclusion, from all peers or by everyone but one peer, followed by an opportunity to act aggressively toward the people who excluded them. The people who acted the least aggressively were the subjects who were accepted by just one person. DeWall states, "Even a glimmer of hope for acceptance can make all the difference."

This glimmer of hope comes in all forms and can even pull people back from a path of aggressive behavior. For example, some police officers in Aarhus, Denmark, have been able to combat the radicalization of youth in their town, who were being targeted by ISIS. They first started hearing about young people disappearing overnight and as they interviewed the parents and community members, they discovered that these Muslim youth were experiencing ongoing rejection and ostracism by their white European neighbors, for both their racial and spiritual differences. The ostracism angered the Muslim youth, making them easy targets for ISIS who promised them a sense of belonging, and as a result, many made the trip to Syria, often disappearing overnight without leaving word with family.

Common practice in most countries was, and is, to declare these people "enemies of the state," treating them like convicted criminals without a charge or a trial. But Danish officers Thorleif Link and Allan Aarslev knew that further societal rejection would only worsen the problem so instead they offered kindness and a path back to being a member of society. They paired people with mentors, helped them find jobs, and in general, extended empathy and kindness. And the results have been astounding. People who had left for Syria came back, cutting their ties to the group. And when the rest of Europe saw a spike in the radicalization of their youth, Aarhus experienced a significant drop.

Now known as "the Aarhus Model," it has become a blueprint for fighting radicalization at its very roots. When people expect to be treated harshly but then are given empathy and kindness, the shock of it causes them to rethink and reevaluate their assumptions about who the enemy really is. And by addressing the real root of societal rejection, the model creates inclusion and belonging.

18. Creating Inclusion

A sense of belonging matters. We don't need to be popular or liked by everyone but we *do* need to have a sense of belonging somewhere, with someone. This has lots of implications for workplaces today. Employee engagement is not just a measure of work pride and productivity, it's also a valuable indicator of inclusion and exclusion. This is why it's so important that measures of engagement include questions like, "Someone at work cares about me as a person," or "I have a friend at work."

This is also why orientation or onboarding efforts are more effective when companies go beyond the basics of new employment and help people integrate socially into their new community. Did you know that one-third of new hires quit their job within six months of starting it? According to a 2014 study by BambooHR, 17 percent said that a friendly smile or a helpful coworker would have made all the difference. Nearly 10 percent wished for more attention from their manager and coworkers.

A study by the Aberdeen Group found that high-performing organizations are two-and-a-half times more likely than lower-performing ones to assign a mentor or buddy during onboarding. This small and affordable effort helps new hires feel connected, plus their experience is seen by someone who can advise and guide them should they hit challenges.

These findings are not a surprise to me. My entire career has focused on the science of success and my doctoral dissertation studied programs and experiences that help people transition to new environments. As a backdrop, I explored Tinto's Model of Student Integration. Dr. Vincent Tinto studied the factors that contributed to college dropout rates and found that students needed to become integrated, a measure of belonging, in both the academic and social environments of their schools. But belonging is a personal perception. One person could have ten friends and feel completely alone while another could have one friend and feel just fine.

In my study, I found that while students needed to reach a certain level of academic integration in order to not flunk out, the social piece was far more impactful. When students didn't find a sense of belonging socially, they were far more likely to leave college as well as experience depression, anxiety, and suicidal thoughts. It turns out that it doesn't matter how old we are or where we are trying to belong, exclusion is harmful. As someone who has run onboarding for both small and large organizations, including a multinational company of 10,000 employees, I can tell you the same is true for new hires. The ability to "find your tribe," even if it's just a tribe of one, can make all the difference. Again, companies with the best new-hire retention purposefully help their newest members navigate the structural and social elements of a new environment.

Case Study: Healthcare Organization
Org Size: Large

"I was hired as the Training Supervisor to oversee the seven-person global training team. My charge was to help them develop consistent skills, manage their performance and behaviors, and increase our support of other units within our organization, especially the call centers that initiate house call visits (HCVs), connecting a clinician to a member in their home.

I was mindful of Tuckman's stages so built the experience to help them work smoothly through each stage in order to build trust with each other and me. We initially had to get to know one another and learn about our personalities and skills while sitting in four different locations around the world. I also had to define their roles and my expectations as a leader of the team so I planned monthly group meetings and weekly one-on-one meetings with each team member. I held two in-person training 'clinics' with the team (one to establish/create training processes, and one on delivery techniques and instructional design concepts).

Through these various sessions, we accomplished several things: role definition, learning about each of our backgrounds (skills, experience, etc.), learning each other's communication styles, understanding how to support and accommodate each other's needs including our 'hot buttons,' and how to best extend common courtesies to each other. We were also working on several key projects together, which helped us become a more tight-knit group.

We achieved and exceeded our goals. We received 90+ requests for training delivery or documentation. We delivered over 500 learning events covering over 50 subjects across the organization; we designed 30+ job aids; and we established 10+

training processes. We helped the call center operators exceed the annual goal of one million scheduled house call visits (usually done by December, it was done by end of September this year!) and their skills improved at all of our locations. We used to be the last thing thought of on a project, but now we get invited to a host of meetings/projects at their inception. This training team received several recognition awards from colleagues and leaders across the organization. In fact, many staff members in other units want to be part of this training team now."

It's worth noting again that belonging is not about being universally liked by everyone. In fact, we each have our own perception of how big our tribe needs to be. But research shows that, at work, what matters most to people is feeling they can make a meaningful contribution and that others value their work. From a tribal perspective, this means they're needed by the group, and therefore, less likely to be ousted. Neurologically, that sense of security is enough to settle the amygdala and allow people to reach higher-order thinking skills like logical analysis and innovation. As we gain more confidence of our position in the group, we perform better. And as we perform better, we gain more confidence.

Some of us find true and deep belonging at work, but most of us really need psychological safety: the ability to make a valuable contribution without fear of being ridiculed or rejected. In addition, we need our colleagues to be more aware of the subtle, and often unintentional ways, they create exclusion through their words and actions. Termed "microaggressions," these are often brief and casual exchanges that send slights, insults or denigrating messages to others based on some aspect of their identity. They are symptoms of unconscious bias because they often are not intended to hurt others, but do so because of their ubiquity and how they accumulate over time to create exclusion. Dr. Derald Wing Sue, author of *Microaggressions in Everyday Life*, argues that there are three distinct forms of microaggressions:

- **Microinsults** (often unconscious): Actions or comments that convey rudeness or insensitivity and demean a person's identity. Examples include assuming criminality based on race (e.g., fear of people of color) or assuming intelligence based on gender (e.g., surprise that a woman is a scientist).

- **Microinvalidations** (often unconscious): Actions or comments that exclude or negate the experience, thoughts or feelings of a person's identity. Examples would include assuming that people of color are immigrants or gay people are taking comments "the wrong way" or are "too sensitive."

- **Microassaults** (often conscious): Intent to hurt others through name-calling, avoidant behavior, or purposefully discriminatory actions. Examples include using insulting terms, or intentionally not hiring people based on their identity.

The challenge with microaggressions is that the targeted groups see and feel them keenly (describing them as repeated stabs or pinpricks) while their colleagues don't see or recognize them as such due to their own cultural blinders, driven by unconscious bias. This can make productive conversations difficult because talking about microaggressions can turn in to interactions filled with microinvalidations unless they are artfully facilitated by skilled professionals.

This is why more and more companies are investing in diversity and inclusion programs that help people move through these difficult but important conversations and shift the focus to be about creating inclusion. As Dr. Christine Cox writes, "Instead of trying to avoid exclusion, we are much better off putting thoughtful effort into enhancing inclusion." Dr. Cox is a researcher at New York University's Langone Medical Center and co-authored a paper titled "The Science of Inclusion: How We Can Leverage the Brain to Build Smarter Teams." Companies like Amazon, Johnson & Johnson, AT&T, Kaiser Permanente, Ernst Young, and eBay are all focusing on creating more inclusive workplaces through efforts like employee resource groups (ERGs), networks, learning experiences, conferences, and leadership development programs. In addition, they are making it a performance marker for managers who have clear diversity and inclusion goals that they are accountable to achieve.

The Role of Empathy

So how do we find our way forward? Through empathy and education. Here is some good news about our brains: We are biologically wired to feel empathy for others as long as we are not in an us-versus-them relationship. Thanks to our mirror neuron system, we feel their social pain as our own. Dr. Giorgia Silani and other neuroscientists used an fMRI machine to explore social pain and they also found that the physical pain region not only lights up for our own exclusion but also when we watch it happen to someone else, "Our data have shown that in conditions of social pain there is activation of an area traditionally associated with the sensory processing of physical pain. This occurred both when the pain was experienced in first person and when the subject experienced it vicariously." Christopher Bergland, a writer for *Psychology Today* observes, "From an evolutionary standpoint, these pain responses protect the individual but also fortify social connectivity which protects the collective."

When we see people as part of our group, we start to neurologically incorporate them into our sense of self. In a study entitled "Familiarity Promotes Blurring of Self and Other in the Neural Representation of Threat," neuroscientists discovered that we become entwined, on a neural level, with people we perceive in our social network of friends and family. "Our self comes to include the people we feel close to. This likely is because humans need to have friends and allies who they can side with and see as being the same as themselves," stated Dr. James Coan.

If you think about it, this aspect of our biology is what allows us to live in communities with each other. Our need to belong, to feel pain when we don't belong, and to experience empathy when we see others in physical or social pain, help us all connect and care for one another in meaningful ways.

Empathy is one of the two core components of psychological safety. Fortunately it can be taught! It is possible, and perhaps should be mandatory, to teach people empathy and other emotional intelligence skills. Even people who are socially challenged, such as people on the autism spectrum, can learn scripts that mimic empathetic responses and when to use them. Well-designed learning events help people develop awareness of and sensitivity to the experiences of others as well as the words and actions that create inclusiveness.

Interestingly, people with a psychopathic personality disorder are known for lacking empathy for others, including lacking remorse when they hurt others, and are often unemotional, callous, and manipulative. Studies at the University of Chicago found that the psychopath's brain responds differently, making their own experience of social pain more intense. In addition, their brain does not activate when seeing another's social or physical pain. In fact, instead, the pleasure part of their brain activates, meaning that they enjoy seeing others suffer. So this group can be resistant to, or even incapable of, developing empathy.

Enhancing Compassion Through Mindfulness

The insular cortex, the brain structure activated by social and physical pain, is made up of two insula, one in each hemisphere, and about the size of a pecan. Studies have shown that the insulae are associated with several functions, including consciousness, emotion, self-awareness, interpersonal connectedness, empathy, and compassion.

New studies are showing that we can alter our insulae through mindfulness. Bergland states in *Psychology Today*, "Neurons in the insula can literally become bulked up and better connected through mindfulness, which can improve the empathetic response of the insula." Dr. Richard Davidson at the University of Wisconsin-Madison has found that those who practiced compassion meditation for 30 minutes a day, for two weeks, were more compassionate in dealing with others. Other studies have also shown that mindfulness can shift how the brain responds to pain, literally creating relief in how we experience and feel both physical and social pain.

Mindfulness may also make us less anxious and reactive. Scientists at Harvard Medical School found that participants who spent close to 30 minutes a day meditating or practicing some other mindfulness activity changed the composition of their amygdala in as little as eight weeks. Scans showed that the physical composition of their brains showed measurable changes, including decreased gray-matter density in the amygdala, which is known to play an important role in anxiety and stress.

The benefits of mindfulness don't stop there. Dr. Davidson recently coauthored the book *Altered Traits: Science Reveals How Meditation Changes Your Mind, Brain, and Body* with Dr. Daniel Goleman, who's considered the "father" of emotional intelligence. As the following empirical study results highlight, this book should be mandatory reading for all humans:

- The amygdala becomes less reactive in as little as 30 hours of mindfulness, shifting people's baseline reactivity by as much as 50 percent. Practitioners can withstand higher levels of pain, have better control over their emotions, and recover more quickly from stressors.

- Meditation practices that focus on compassion and loving-kindness can show results in as little as 8 hours. More impressively, Davidson and Goleman state, "Reductions in usually intractable unconscious bias emerge after just 16 hours." More time yields stronger results.

- Mindfulness immediately quiets the constant internal narrative we have about ourselves—that part of our brain that ruminates about the past and worries about the future. While the effect is an immediate by-product of the practice itself, it can become an enduring state with long-term practice.

- In as little as three-days of mindfulness training, the body reduces its production of pro-inflammatory cytokines, which create inflammation. Extensive practice shifts this to become an enduring physical trait. In as little as three months of an intensive mindfulness practice, the body increases its production of the telomerase enzyme, which slows cellular aging. Yes, you read that right—you can get younger!

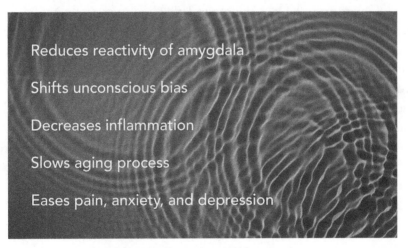

Reduces reactivity of amygdala

Shifts unconscious bias

Decreases inflammation

Slows aging process

Eases pain, anxiety, and depression

The benefits of a regular mindfulness practice

- Mindfulness has been shown to reduce a range of mental health challenges including depression, anxiety, and pain—to the same level as prescription medications but without the side effects. Loving-kindness meditation seems especially effective for people who have experienced trauma and those with post-traumatic stress disorder.

The authors are quick to point out that these effects vary based on the intensity and duration of the practice. They detail studies that involve first-time meditators, quasiregular practitioners, and people who have spent a lifetime of deep devotion to the tradition. One life-long practitioner had spent 62,000 hours meditating—his 41-year-old brain looked like that of a 33-year-old.

While you may not have a goal to embrace an intensive practice, it is clear that we all can stand to gain quite a few positive benefits from beginning a practice and sticking with it. Newbies may see and feel differences in as little as two weeks. This was certainly true for me. I do a light practice using the *21-Day Meditation Experience* by Deepak Chopra and Oprah Winfrey. These ten-minute sessions are organized around a theme and available on a smartphone app, making them the perfect thing for my life. At work, I love to use the short work-related meditations on Desk-Yogi.com. There are many levels and types of mindfulness supports out there, including meditation groups that meet online or in person. And many companies are starting to provide classes and group sessions on a range of mindfulness practices.

Goleman and Davidson found that long-term meditators, who have done 1,000-plus hours, experience more robust benefits, with mindfulness helping them to develop enduring traits rather than a state achieved for a short amount of time. Finally, Davidson's research of yogis' brains (defined as people with more than 27,000 hours of practice) found that they achieve unique brain patterns not seen in other people, particularly in their gamma waves and neural synchrony. This pattern is amplified during meditation but endures throughout the rest of their day. The result seems to be that this slows the aging of their brains, something clearly noticeable on fMRI and EEG scans.

19. Finding True Belonging

For years, workplace focus on diversity often consisted of forcing employees to sit through mandatory trainings that were not well designed nor facilitated. While the intention was positive, the effects were often less so, sometimes causing more tension and misunderstandings.

The goal today is inclusion, where people feel that the can bring their whole selves to work. Vernā Myers states "Diversity is being invited to the party; inclusion is being asked to dance." While workplaces are certainly more diverse than they were even a couple of decades ago, we still have a long way to go.

In a study published in *Harvard Business Review*, researchers Kenji Yoshino and Christie Smith discovered that nearly two-thirds of employees "feel pressure to 'cover' some facet of their identity at work." In their assessment, hiding or covering was particularly true of these groups:

- 83 percent of lesbian/gay/bisexual workers
- 79 percent of blacks
- 66 percent of women
- 63 percent of Hispanics
- 61 percent of Asians
- 45 percent of heterosexual, white men (who often felt they had to cover their age and physical disabilities, including mental health)

2/3 of employees feel pressure to "cover" some facet of their identity at work

The majority of employees feel pressure to hide aspects of themselves

They have coauthored a report titled *Uncovering Talent: A New Model of Inclusion*. In it, they identify four axes along which people might feel they need to cover to protect their long-term professional advancement:

- **Appearance-based:** How individuals alter their self-presentation—including grooming, attire, and mannerisms—to blend into the mainstream. For instance, a black woman might straighten her hair to deemphasize her race.

- **Affiliation-based:** How individuals avoid behaviors widely associated with their identity, often to negate stereotypes about that identity. A woman might avoid talking about being a mother because she does not want her colleagues to think she is less committed to her work or a Latino man might talk less about his weekend activities because he doesn't want to be perceived as "lazy."

- **Advocacy-based:** How much individuals "stick up for" their group. A veteran might refrain from challenging a joke about the military, lest they be seen as overly strident.

- **Association-based:** How individuals avoid contact with other group members. A gay person might refrain from bringing his same-sex partner to a work function to avoid being perceived as "too gay."

Covering up takes people's time and energy, as they work to not reveal their authentic selves by altering what they wear, say, and act. Clearly, this is an indicator that people already feel excluded or fear further marginalization. This can lead to wasting people's talents and ultimately impacts the success of the organizations for whom they work. Another way to consider this is to ask yourself how much more productive your organization would be if 60 percent of your talent wasn't spending precious energy on covering themselves at work. Again, psychological safety is the antidote, making its value even stronger.

Neurologically, when people feel they are valued and needed by a group, the brain produces serotonin, and can shift from reptilian/survival brain to the neocortex, which is the seat of innovation and other higher-order thinking. Clearly, psychologically unsafe organizations are at a continual and increasing competitive disadvantage.

As we've seen, inclusion and belonging drive health and happiness as well as psychological safety. There's really no downside to that in the workplace. Researcher Dr. Brené Brown explored these themes in her book *Braving the Wilderness: The Quest for True Belonging and the Courage to Stand Alone*. She studied people who seem to have found true belonging to see what set them apart. She provides this definition:

> Belonging is the innate human desire to be part of something larger than us. Because this yearning is so primal, we often try to acquire it by fitting in and by seeking approval, which are not only hollow substitutes for belonging, but often barriers to it. Because true belonging only happens when we present our authentic, imperfect selves to the world, our sense of belonging can never be greater than our level of self-acceptance. True belonging doesn't require you to change who you are; it requires you to be who are you.

She found that, to develop true belonging, we must be able develop trust, with others and ourselves. It's no surprise that trust is also a key differentiator of the top performing teams and the healthiest organizations. Let's dig in a little deeper to see why.

20. The Power of Trust and Purpose

Patrick Lencioni, an internationally recognized expert on teams, states "Teamwork begins by building trust. And the only way to do that is to overcome our need for invulnerability."

According to the PricewaterhouseCoopers *20th Global CEO Survey*, 55 percent of CEOs think that a lack of trust is a threat to their organization's growth.

The Great Place to Work organization puts trust at the center of its model, as the element from which the rest of an organization's culture grows. In their report *The Business Case for a High-Trust Culture*, they share several studies that show that trust drives better employee engagement and retention, higher customer satisfaction, better innovation, faster agility, and ultimately more productivity and profit. In fact, high-trust companies experience 50 percent less turnover and double or triple the stock market returns. According to their thirty-plus years of research, "employees experience high levels of trust when they believe these things:

1. Leaders are credible (based on competence, communication, honesty).
2. They are treated with respect as people and professionals.
3. The workplace is fundamentally fair."

I suspect that these elements also create the conditions for psychological safety and inclusion because they grow out of respect and fairness. Neurologically, these elements—credible leaders, respectful treatment, and fairness—combine to help employees move from their reptilian/survival brain to operate more often and consistently in the neocortex or higher thinking parts of the brain.

The Brain Science of Trust

Neuroscientist Dr. Paul Zak of the Center for Neuroeconomic Studies, has been studying trust in the workplace for years. While we all instinctively know that trust is a positive factor, his research has helped him identify a mathematical relationship between trust and economic performance. Simply, more trust equals better performance.

He wanted to explore more deeply what signals to us that someone is trustworthy. He built upon others' research that found that mammal brains produce a neurotransmitter called oxytocin, which signals that another animal is safe to approach. You may have heard about oxytocin in the news. It's the same chemical that aids parents in bonding with their children as the brain releases a flood of it during childbirth and nursing. We also produce more of it when we hug and kiss others, especially in relation to consensual romantic and sexual encounters. In fact, it's been nicknamed "the love hormone" because of the role it plays in our closest relationships. Dr. Shelley Taylor, of UCLA's Social Neuroscience Lab, has labeled it the "tend and befriend" response, which makes it markedly different from our "fight or flight" response. Some scientists say it helps us shift from struggle to snuggle.

Oxytocin is produced in the thalamus and then released through the pituitary gland into our blood stream. There are oxytocin receptors through our central nervous system and when oxytocin binds with them, it influences our physiology making us feel calmer, happier, and more trusting.

This influence certainly affects us in the moment, but more importantly, it can also alter us for a lifetime. Separate studies at the Universities of California and Wisconsin have shown that babies (both humans and other mammals) who reach certain levels and duration of oxytocin in their youth (through bonding), go on to be more able to bond with others and build trust as they get older. This confirms evidence from adoptive parents whose children come from orphanages where little touching or holding occurred. Psychologists have long known that children who grow up in abusive or neglectful environments often struggle to form close relationships with others throughout their lives.

Oxytocin can also counterbalance the stress of exclusion. Scientists at the University of Illinois at Chicago gave animals who had been isolated for an extended time and were showing signs of anxiety, depression, and cardiac stress, either doses of oxytocin or saline. The animals that received the oxytocin no longer showed signs of any of the symptoms.

Dr. Paul Zak has found that oxytocin is a fairly accurate measure of trust. He has measured oxytocin in humans both in laboratory studies as well as real workplaces. For example, in the lab, he took blood samples from subjects both before and after participating in an activity where they either had to extend trust to someone or were on the receiving end of that trust. For the receivers, oxytocin levels increased from the initial blood draw. In addition, higher levels of oxytocin in the initial blood measurement accurately predicted how much trust participants would extend.

Increasing the dose increased the actions of trust. This effect centered solely on actions between people, something they tested by giving subjects a gambling task to test if it indicated a lowering of general inhibition. It did not. Zak states, "Oxytocin appeared to do just one thing—reduce the fear of trusting a stranger."

In fact, its effect is so powerful, it can impact long-standing and intractable relationships. A study by Dr. Simone Shamay-Tsoory found that giving oxytocin increased empathy between Israeli-Jewish and Palestinian subjects. The results are detailed in the article, "Giving Peace a Chance: Oxytocin Increases Empathy to Pain in the Context of the Israeli-Palestinian Conflict."

Zak has spent the last decade studying trust in organizations, which he details in his book *Trust Factor: The Science of Creating High-Performance Companies*. He conducted numerous studies in a variety of workplaces around the world. Here are some of the key findings from his research:

- The relationship between trust and oxytocin is universal spanning cultures, races and geographic regions.
- Oxytocin increases a person's empathy to others.
- High-stress environments inhibit oxytocin production, with stressed people less effectively able to interact with others.
- People at high-trust companies are healthier with 74 percent less stress and 13 percent fewer sick days. They also have 106 percent more energy at work and 40 percent less burnout.
- People at high-trust companies feel 66 percent closer to their colleagues and have 11 percent more empathy for them.
- A sense of purpose promotes oxytocin production.

Building Trust

Trust is not something that is built overnight. Nor can you just claim that you are trustworthy. The world is filled with leaders who claim to be competent or trustworthy but their daily actions show that they are not. Biologically, we watch for and respond to actions, not words. Trust is earned, not proclaimed.

Doctors Jim Kouzes and Barry Posner, authors of *The Leadership Challenge*, identified this 25 years ago when they researched what differentiated the best leaders from the rest. Leaders walk their talk and by consistently demonstrating their values, integrity and commitment, they build their credibility and earn the trust of their followers.

Dr. Brené Brown says that trust is built in those small moments where, over time, we learn we can count on each other. She likens it to putting marbles in a jar. When we have enough marbles in that jar, we can withstand a few withdrawals—disagreements, conflicts, or mistakes where we inadvertently do something that upsets or harms another.

But what is trust exactly? Seasoned business coach, Charles Feltman, defines trust as "choosing to risk making something you value vulnerable to another person's actions," in his book *The Thin Book of Trust: An Essential Primer for Building Trust at Work*. He argues that trust is built and also lost in our daily interactions. Specifically, he finds that trust centers around these four elements:

1. Sincerity: A person means what they say and acts accordingly
2. Reliability: A person consistently delivers what they promised
3. Competence: A person is clear about what they can and cannot do
4. Care: A person takes the "we" perspective and has both your interest as well as theirs in mind

As you can see, trust naturally activates a sense of we. It's clear from the research that all of the benefits of healthy groups and teams live in that sense of we. And in fact, very harmful effects happen when we go past "we" to "us versus them."

Damien Hooper-Campbell, eBay's first chief diversity officer, talks about redrawing our "circles of trust." He argues that we all have circles of trust that people in our lives have earned the right to be in. But at work, we can spend hours with people and not really get to know them. He argues that organizations should be focusing on drawing wider circles faster to help people have those important conversations and interactions that will let them trust each other.

Dr. Brené Brown further teases out building trust to seven elements that create the acronym BRAVING.

- Boundaries: We define our boundaries and communicate those to others. We respect people's boundaries. We are willing to say no.
- Reliability: We deliver—not only what we promised but in our accurate assessment of our competencies and priorities, so that we don't make commitments we can't keep.

- Accountability: We take responsibility for our mistakes, apologize, and do what we can to make things right.
- Vault: We keep confidences; we do not share what is not ours to share.
- Integrity: We show our values through our daily actions and practices. We walk the walk, and not just talk the talk.
- Nonjudgment: We can ask for what we need and talk about our feelings without judging others.
- Generosity: We extend the most generous interpretation possible to the intentions, words, and actions of others. We assume best intent.

These elements arose from her data as she talked to hundreds of people about both resilience (in her book *Rising Strong*) and also belonging (*Braving the Wilderness*). She argues that they can help us both create trust with others and also with ourselves. Together, these elements contribute to trust and psychological safety, naturally helping groups and teams achieve that sense of we.

Harnessing Purpose

In his numerous studies, Dr. Paul Zak found that a sense of purpose stimulates oxytocin, stating, "Experiments show that having a sense of higher purpose stimulates oxytocin production, as does trust. Trust and purpose mutually reinforce each other, providing a mechanism for extended oxytocin release, which produces happiness. So, joy on the job comes from doing purpose-driven work with a trusted team."

When I read that, I had one of those profound "aha!" moments where everything becomes crystal clear. This is THE THING that explains my own professional career and why I thrived in some places and struggled in others. Looking back on it, I felt most engaged, happiest, and productive when doing purpose-driven work with colleagues I trusted.

I'm not the only one. In his best-selling book *The Purpose Economy*, economist Aaron Hurst argues that purpose is the fourth great American economy, the first three being agrarian, industrial, and information. According to Hurst, purpose lives at the intersection of what gives us meaning and the impact we want to have. According to his global study, 40 percent of US workers are purpose-oriented, meaning that it's their primary reason for working. This doesn't mean the rest are slackers, just that they prioritize status or money as their *primary* reason for working (but many of whom still express their sense of purpose in their personal lives through hobbies and volunteerism). The rise of the purpose-driven employee is a global phenomenon, representing 37 percent of the global workforce—Sweden is the highest at 53 percent and Saudi Arabia the lowest at 23 percent.

Hurst argues that purpose-driven employees create all kinds of benefits for organizations. As he puts it, "People who work with purpose have better relationships, greater impact, and greater growth." In the *2015 Global Purpose Index*, Hurst found that purpose-driven workers have 64 percent higher levels of fulfillment in their work, are 50 percent more likely to be in leadership positions, and 47 percent more likely to recommend their place of work to others.

He also carefully demystifies purpose, claiming that it's not about working for a cause or only something that Millennials care about. It's not purpose with a capital P, but a little p: what's unique to each of us, that intersection of what gives us meaning and where we can make the most impact. Purpose fuels motivation, helping us persist when things get challenging. It's a counterweight to the stress that fills so much of today's workplaces. In addition, my research found that purpose plays a key role neurologically, providing all kinds of benefits like better cognitive resilience, slowing age-related decline, and reducing depression.

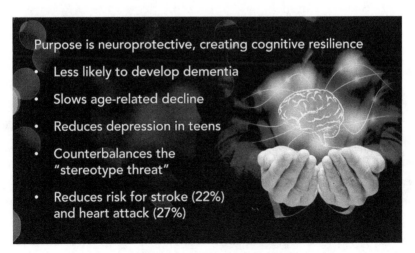

The neuroprotective properties of purpose

As we saw in studies in the previous section, purpose can also counterbalance the threat of stereotyping. When people focus on what they find meaningful, it moves them back into their thinking brain and allows them to perform at their normal or even best levels. Purpose also helps people survive the most terrible of traumas and atrocities. Dr. Victor Frankl, a physician trained in psychiatry and neurology, was also a Holocaust survivor. In his seminal book *Man's Search for Meaning*, he states, "There is nothing in the world that would so effectively help one to survive even the worst conditions as the knowledge that there is a meaning in one's life."

What does this all mean for teams in today's workplaces? Inclusion is vitally necessary if we want to bring out the best in people. More importantly, any form of exclusion is painful, and incredibly damaging to individuals, the teams they are on, and the organizations they work for. Long-term rejection can fuel disengagement, apathy, aggression, and even extreme violence.

Whereas inclusion only brings benefits. Dr. Christine Cox, in her research at New York University's Langone School of Medicine, has identified six areas that are enhanced by inclusion and worsened by exclusion. They are:

- Intelligent thought and reasoning
- Self-care and self-improvement
- Prosocial behavior
- Self-regulation
- A sense of purpose
- Well-being

Needless to say, each of these items represents real financial gains or losses for teams and organizations.

Inclusion can be created and enhanced through some relatively simple practices. Moving people to a sense of we happens through empathy, something that can be both taught and enhanced during learning experiences and through mindfulness. Trust is a biological process that can likewise be built and strengthened between people. And making a sense of purpose a priority can unite and enliven a diverse group of people, driving all kinds of positive effects for teams and organizations.

Your Learning Journey

Consider how the brain science of trust and inclusion impacts you.

- We all have experienced exclusion or rejection at some point. Jot down some notes about what happened and how it impacted you.
- Identify the people and groups that make you feel included. What do they do and say to make you feel like you belong?
- In what ways have you had to cover yourself at work? Which of the four types did you experience?
- Reflect on a team experience where you had high trust. How did people express the BRAVING elements?
- What is the meaningful purpose that motivates you? How can you bring more of it into your teams and workplace?

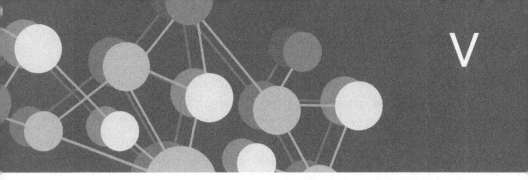

A NEW MODEL: THE FOUR GATES TO PEAK TEAM PERFORMANCE™

"Trust and purpose mutually reinforce each other, providing a mechanism for extended oxytocin release, which produces happiness. So, joy on the job comes from doing purpose-driven work with a trusted team."

Dr. Paul Zak, *The Trust Factor*

21. A New Team Model

As I looked at the research on the brain science of groups and teams, I envisioned a new model clearly emerge that honors our biological processes (the way our human brains and bodies naturally sort). It also gives us insight into how we can enhance team performance to foster the fullest potential of each team and its members. My model also distinguishes between different levels of performance, articulating the difference between a medium-performing team and one that excels. Finally, it clearly shows why you cannot get to the highest level of peak performance without certain things in place.

When I did this research, I had many moments of insight that explained my own best and worst team experiences. We all hunger to be part of a group. We seek this on a deep, core level, and when we find it, we thrive. Many of us have been lucky enough to experience that in the workplace and when it happens, it is *truly* special. My fondest memories and best performances so far have been when I was doing meaningful work with a trusted team. Other times, I'd been doing okay but now know something was missing, something vital that I yearned for. As so many of us have experienced, even viscerally, it's that magical, unknown quality that makes the best teams different from the rest.

But now we have pinpointed that magical quality.

As I work with other organizations and groups, I see this too. Certain teams have that special sauce that make them amazing, while others (who might even sit ten feet away) don't. It's also in the stories scattered throughout this book. These real case studies of teams that succeed and teams that struggle can all be mapped to this new model I've developed. Let's explore it now.

Energy Drains and Boosters

The data is clear that we are wired to connect with others and when we do, both teams and individuals can perform at their fullest potential. When conditions are right, we can align quickly, communicate effectively, learn from each other, and access the highest levels of our thinking and decision making.

Many aspects of our biology are designed to help us connect with others, but lots of things can get in the way. We only truly connect when we are safe enough to do so—in other words, when we don't feel threatened, physically or psychologically. That seems to be a mandatory condition to bring our whole selves to work and to perform at our best. The safer we feel, the better we perform. Biologically, we can access more of our higher thinking functions and we don't waste energy on constantly scanning our environment and protecting ourselves.

So one key element of helping teams thrive is to increase safety or, as the case may be, reduce threat. For every element of threat, we can anticipate a corresponding drop in potential or performance. I would argue that today people come to work and perform at half to a third of their potential, perhaps even less, because of the prevalence of these typical workplace threats:

- Aggression and violence
- Bullying and harassment
- Stereotypes and discrimination (sexism, racism, etc.)
- Exclusion and ostracism

Threats may come from any level of an organization. For example, you may feel great on your immediate team but feel a threat from your supervisor or a colleague in another department. Senior leaders may also be threats, in their own behavior or by condoning the behavior of others. The most powerful threats are the closest ones, so our immediate supervisor's behavior will likely have more impact than a more distant leader but an executive can still terrorize an entire organization.

Dealing with threats requires energy—physical, mental, and emotional. The more energy a team's individual people are using to deal with threats, the less they have available to bring their best effort to work. Picture people as vessels of energy and threats to them like a drain, slowing leaking energy away. In other words, depending on the number and type of imminent threats, people operate at various levels of their potential. Some have a full tank, while others are at 50 percent, and some might be at 20 percent.

When people come together in a team, their energy levels combine. If most of Team A's members run at full energy, you might anticipate they will perform better than Team B, whose members operate at a half or quarter potential. Team B might still do great things but whatever they accomplish will be a fraction of what they were capable of. No wonder Google spent millions studying teams. More teams achieving peak performance translates to more organizational success in every metric that matters.

It's clear that we need to pay attention to the safety of each individual team member as well as the safety of the combined team. And remove as many threats as possible.

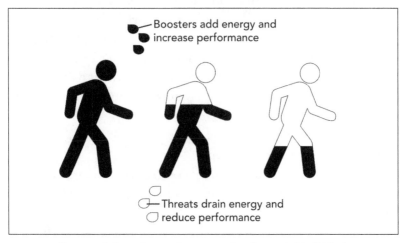

Boosts and threats impact the energy and performance of individuals

While threats may drain energy, other things can enhance it: a strong sense of personal purpose, close relationships with others, and a regular mindfulness practice may help people perform better, or mitigate some of the threats' impacts. Enhancers—or, boosters—increase energy or capacity, instead of draining it away.

As we saw in the last section, purpose can have a strong influence on individuals and teams. More and more people (25 to 50 percent) are motivated by purpose, and when an organization's or team's purpose and an individual's purpose align, it can be an extra energy boost, which can overcome or counterbalance some of the energy lost in other areas. In fact, people will often endure negative team environments because they believe so strongly in the mission or purpose of the task or the organization.

Working adults have another layer of purpose, in choosing careers and jobs where we can spend time doing what matters to us. Some of us love to help others so choose work that gives us lots of contact with and impact on people. Others prefer working with objects and things. Some love conceptual work, others are hands-on. Regardless of the form, most of us seek to express our inner sense of purpose through our work. Even people who feel they have limited options, for example aging or uneducated workers, still make choices on where to apply and what to accept among their alternatives.

Some people use their jobs to fund their "true" purpose outside of work. This might be time with family, supporting a meaningful cause, or spending time on something engrossing and fun. So even though they don't love their work per se, it provides a means to a meaningful end for them.

While boosters vary by individual, they can also be part of the work environment. For example, an inspiring leader might motivate employees to be excited about an organization and its mission. Having a good group of trusted friends at work can also be a booster. So can receiving recognition and financial and other rewards.

It's safe to say that boosters positively impact everyone, raising performances across the board. For people experiencing threats, boosters may counterbalance drains that may be keeping them from performing at a high or even satisfactory level. But the organizations that see the biggest results are the ones who actively reduce all threats *while* also enabling and enhancing boosters.

22. The Four Gates to Peak Team Performance

The brain science of teams shows that there's a natural progression through a threat-assessment process that unfolds over time. Before we can operate at our highest level and fullest potential, we must first address threats. Then we can explore and embrace positive elements of connection.

Remember, we are wired to survive, belong, and become. In that order. Always.

As we join a team and engage with teammates, we assess the potential threats and respond accordingly. I see each stage much like a gate; once we go through it, a whole new level opens up. For example, when we sort for friend or foe, our biology responds accordingly, either shifting into fight-flight-freeze survival mode or moving on to sorting for me and we.

At each of the four gates, our (largely unconscious) scans help us determine our context. We ask ourselves a few key questions and assign a rating. Ultimately, these become an indicator of the amount of drain we experience at that gate. If things are good, our energy stays intact; if things are challenging, we experience drain, unless counterbalanced by a booster.

The four gates are safety, purpose, belonging, and peak performance. Teams cannot achieve peak performance without first establishing sufficient levels of the first three elements. As we progress through the four gates, we lose, maintain, or gain energy that ultimately determines our individual performance as well as the overall team's performance. So, the gates represent levels of *potential* for peak performance. The more energy you lose at each gate, the less likely the team can achieve peak performance. And conversely, the more energy maintained or gained, the more likely the team can achieve their fullest potential.

I'm going to first describe the four gates and then I will illustrate them by comparing two teams.

Gate 1: Safety

It should be no surprise that safety is the first gate. The very core of our biology focuses on survival and any threat is bad. At this gate we scan for four main threats:

1.   Threats of physical harm and aggression

2. Bullying and harassment
3. Threats to our livelihood/career and perceived job security (which allows us to purchase food, water, and shelter)
4. Rejection or exclusion from the group (since that is also a threat to our survival)

The unspoken questions we unconsciously ask ourselves center around how likely we are to experience the following:

- Am I safe from physical harm?
- Will I be harassed or bullied?
- Could I be punished by being demoted, sidelined, or fired?
- Will I be rejected by or excluded from the group?

In essence, we assess or rate the likelihood that we will experience these threats to our safety, almost like moving levers on a continuum from extremely likely to unlikely. This invisible scoreboard becomes an internal rating of our safety.

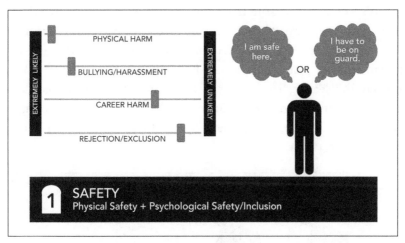

Gate 1: Safety

As a team initially comes together, people naturally scan for these issues. We assess the various members of the team including the leader. The team leader is often the supervisor and teammates are often immediate colleagues, but not always. In today's work world it's very likely that people are on several teams, either serially or simultaneously. Each category of threat represents a potential energy drain. If we assess that a threat is unlikely, we keep our energy. But each level of likelihood means we will be spending time scanning for, and protecting ourselves from, possible threats. We decide if we are safe or need to be on guard.

At this first gate, we use our initial interactions to determine how safe we feel, physically and psychologically. You'll notice that the first half of Edmondson's definition of psychological safety lives at this level; "A sense of confidence that the team will not embarrass, reject, or punish someone for speaking up with ideas, questions, concerns or mistakes." The other half comes in at a later gate.

This gate aligns with Tuckman's stage of forming where people come together and start to learn about the task and each other. First impressions matter; how we bring teams together and support their initial interactions can be helpful, neutral, or harmful. For example, a teammate's ill-timed comment or action at this delicate time can set people on a path of wariness and distrust that is not easily overcome. Put another way, at this gate, we don't have any marbles in our marble jar—the experiences that build trust—so we are at our most sensitive level of threat detection and reactivity. In addition, if threatening behavior is ignored or condoned by the leader, it adds a secondary layer of threat.

It's important to note that at this stage, even if they have detected several potential threats, people will often continue on with a team, most often because the project might be mandatory. If there is not enough trust in place, people simply won't speak up, so an outsider, or even the leader, might not detect anything wrong. People may outwardly exhibit signs that things are fine and try to get along with everyone, while, internally, the survival brain is activated, draining precious energy away.

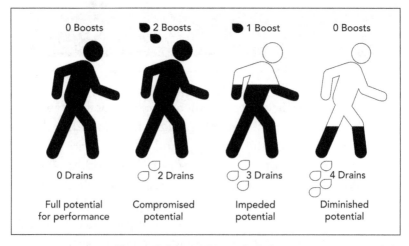

Team with drains and boosts from Gate 1

As team members move toward the second gate, they perform at the levels of their potential, depending on how much energy is draining away with or without any boosts. Some people might feel great about the group, not detecting any threats and operating at full capacity. Others might feel anything from mild to serious threat levels.

It's should be no surprise, then, that a team with more collective energy will likely perform better than another group with less. But whatever energy they have at this point, they now enter the second gate.

Gate 2: Purpose

The second gate focuses on purpose. Every organization has a purpose and teams are often formed to accomplish various aspects of the vision and mission. When a team is brought together, there is something to be done—a purpose to be achieved—that requires the contributions of more than one person.

Like the first gate, we do some assessments of our context along a few criteria, this time focused on clarity. In this gate, it's the following four areas in terms of our likelihood:

1. Achieving clarity on the task/purpose
2. Ability to succeed in accomplishing the task/purpose
3. Being able to contribute our strengths
4. Feel aligned and connected with others

What is the goal of the team's work together? Is the purpose clearly articulated by the leader and understood by the group? Lack of clarity or understanding creates a threat or drain when people are unsure how the group will be able to succeed.

Next, we assess the likelihood of success. Knowing you've been tasked with something you might not be able to accomplish is disheartening (and draining). A variety of factors play a role here:

- A deadline that is difficult, if not impossible, to hit
- Lack of resources needed to complete at the expected level of quality
- Unskilled, uninformed, or incompetent teammates
- Ineffective leadership
- A constraining culture or context

History in an organization also impacts this assessment, especially negatively. If we have been part of several teams that did not get the necessary resources or had ineffective leadership, we are likely to anticipate the same and move our levers, so to speak, to the "unlikely" side of the continuum.

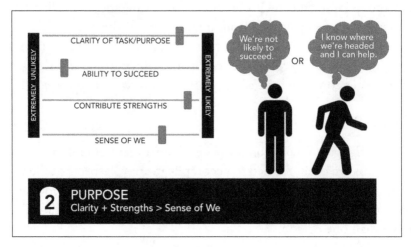

Gate 2: Purpose

In the third continuum on our "purpose meter" we assess how likely we are to be enabled to make a valuable contribution to the team/project. Being able to contribute is a primary biological need because it helps us secure our place within the group. People often feel anxious or worried if they don't see an opportunity to contribute and feel excited and motivated if they do.

To this end, working professionals really want to be allowed to use their strengths at work. Research by Gallup has found that employees who can use their strengths at work are six times more likely to be engaged than workers who cannot. They also perform better and are less likely to leave their company.

These elements help build the sense of we, the final assessment of this gate. When people feel they can make a meaningful contribution to something achievable, it creates a sense of connection to the team and organization. This is not yet true belonging but it's a precursor to it.

As we learned earlier, we naturally sort for whether we are an individual or part of a collective. This gate pushes people one direction or the other, so it is a critical part of the team's process. Leaders play a vital role at this gate and can greatly help or hinder the assessments each individual is making and the team's overall process.

As team members move toward the third gate, the energy drains and boosts from this gate add to what was accrued or lost from the first. Again, the team's potential is made up of the potential of each individual member.

Gate 2 aligns with Tuckman's storming and norming stages as well as skills for cooperation and coordination. It's important to note that these gates overlap, and crossing through one doesn't mean that you're done with those issues. Threats to our safety, such as harassment or bullying, can crop up anytime, and when they do we experience the additional drain even if we're on to another gate.

The gates mirror our biological process, in order, as we meet others and form a group. Again, the overall, collective energy of the team impacts their ability to perform at their full potential. They turn toward the third gate with the combined/accumulated drains and boosts of the first two gates.

Case Study: Nuclear Power Company
Org Size: Medium

"Our team was responsible for driving learning and training across the company. The company does not operate an organizational development department, nor really what I would call a learning and development department. Training in the company was very much a compliance-based, check-the-box kind of culture. We were less a team than a department that was missing purpose, vision, mission, and goals. We eventually stated our 2017 vision (in August) as promoting a culture of learning.

Our manager had a reputation for being resistant to change. I was the new person, and admittedly innovative. I'm also quite strategic and used to working with executive teams. When I would promote new ideas, I'd be met with skepticism and/or flat-out nos. I would be told by colleagues to not even bother trying. I would implore for strategic thinking to still push ideas through... colleagues would continue to tell me it wasn't going to happen and the manager was just getting mad at me. At times, nothing would come of it (i.e., idea squashed or I failed to negotiate initiative) but sometimes the idea would suddenly be happening and our VP was impressed with our 'manager's idea.' Ouch!

Teaming was not happening. There was very little trust and very little collaboration. We were siloed in our own department.

Thus, making the idea of 'building a culture of learning' near impossible. Employees were cynical and unmotivated. They didn't believe any 'new' ideas were worth sharing, as they'd 'never get approved.' I was laughed at when optimistic about a new idea. I was regularly told that the org would 'beat me down, eventually.'

Ultimately the lack of trust, safety, micromanagement, and poor communication led to our administrative assistant quitting. Well, actually she refused to go to meetings or do her job anymore, threatened to quit, but was ultimately let go. I've never witnessed the degradation of a person's demeanor and it shocked me. She went from being a sweet person to a cynical, mean person completely devoid of self-confidence.

The organization seems to have no desire to address the real issues. Conflict is avoided or suppressed and the team has a fear of authenticity or vulnerability. As a result, we have not really achieved any team goals. Three people quit in less than a year, all stating it's due to the manager. I'm the only one left and I'm leaving soon too because I have to be in a place where I can thrive. The last one standing will be the boss. The lonely boss, wondering why the team all left. The lack of self-awareness may not allow looking into the mirror."

Gate 3: Belonging

At the third gate we have the opportunity to move into true belonging and the full definition of psychological safety.

We have come through the gates of safety and purpose and continue to experience the drains of any threats we encountered there. As a result, we may or may not be able to fully harvest this gate's benefits if we are too burdened from deficits at the previous two. In addition, the third gate must score toward "extremely likely" each of its assessments in order to move to the fourth and final gate.

This third gate is about the elements humans need to feel truly and authentically part of team and therefore able to do the more difficult work of collaboration. It aligns with Tuckman's stage of performing but only when teams hit sufficient levels of likelihood for the various assessments at this gate. The assessments of Gate 3 are:

1. Being respected or valued by the group

2. The amount of trust that exists
3. Feeling safe enough to take risks and make mistakes
4. Ability to resolve conflict effectively

The first assessment at this gate is how respected or valued we feel by the group. Biologically, being valued gives us a sense of protection—that we matter enough to greatly reduce our chance of exclusion. Respect is a bit different (you can be valued but not respected and vice versa) but it's also a measure of esteem within the group and also offers protection. Like protection, being valued and respected can make us feel like we belong—that we matter to others in a meaningful way.

Next, we evaluate how much we trust others. At this point in a team's time together, members should have had enough interactions that they can assess how much trust others have earned. This is easier if few threats or drains occurred at the previous gates; or if there were threats but people have put time and energy into developing their relationships. This is where the number of marbles in the jar matters. There needs to be quite a few marbles to give this a positive assessment but it's never too late to add/earn them.

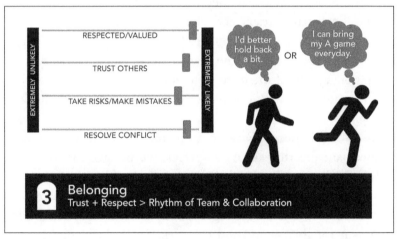

Gate 3: Belonging

Psychological safety appears again at this gate but now it's the second part of Edmondson's definition: "It is a shared belief that the team is safe for interpersonal risk-taking. It describes a team climate characterized by interpersonal trust and mutual respect in which people are comfortable being themselves." People feel that they can take risks and make mistakes because they know that they are truly safe to do so.

They can reveal parts of themselves, beyond just taking risks with work projects, removing whatever masks or covers they have been wearing to be their authentic selves. This acts as a boost because it frees up energy that was previously being used to maintain an "appropriate" or "professional" image. That's not to say that people become un-professional but rather they are more authentic and vulnerable with each other.

Finally, people assess how likely it is that the team can work through conflict. As we learned earlier, true collaboration requires skills for conflict resolution and the group needs to feel a certain level of confidence that conflicts can be worked through effectively. This allows people to tussle with the creative tensions that occur in collaboration, knowing that respect and trust can be maintained, or even enhanced as they do so. In addition, people need to know that conflicts won't have lasting effects or consequences on their relationships and place within the group.

Each person's unconscious assessments contribute to whether they feel like they can lean in to the team and their role or if they had better maintain some self-protection. When the assessments are pos-itive, people often feel that they can now really bring their A-game to work. Potential barriers and challenges to peak performance are removed and momentum can really start to gather. In addition, conditions are in place for the team to drop into neural synchrony, making the rhythm of the team faster and easier. It's a like a well-oiled machine where the work can feel effortless even when it's difficult or challenging.

Gate 3 is special because it is the zone of both incredible happiness and heartbreak. As a species, we hunger for this sense of belonging. It's what Paul Zak talks about when he says, "Joy on the job comes from doing meaningful work with a trusted team." When we have this experience, it's highly motivating. People feel pride and enthusiasm for their work, and care deeply for their colleagues. As a result, they often go above and beyond what is expected, becoming the highly engaged workers that Gallup talks about.

While we all want this kind of belonging, it's a somewhat rare experience. It can be hard for teams to get to this level but even when they do, a change in a leader or a couple members of the team can shift the dynamic. While it can be regained, it takes time. And once you have known this kind of team experience, it can be heartbreaking to lose it.

In fact, some people spend their careers trying to achieve it or find it again. To date, it has not been an easy thing to replicate because it's the culmination of all the pieces that came before, including the unique contributions of each person as well as their individual and collective threats and boosts.

With this model and the key practices and strategies I'll share in the next section, we can create and recreate this kind of team experience. The answers lie in our biology and honoring the natural process our bodies are already using to engage with others.

Only teams in the best shape can enter the fourth and final gate, the one that represents peak performance.

Gate 4: Peak Performing

Few groups cross the fourth gate, but those that do enter a state of incredibly high performance and fulfilled potential. A team at this level is so connected and aligned that they are able to consistently engage in creative and innovative work, taking appropriate risks and learning from each experience.

Nothing is held back; every person brings their full capacity, with a harmonious cadence that makes working together almost effortless and which makes challenging tasks seem achievable, even easy. This team also has a lot of fun together and genuinely like each other. They may or may not socialize outside of work but create an authentic camaraderie.

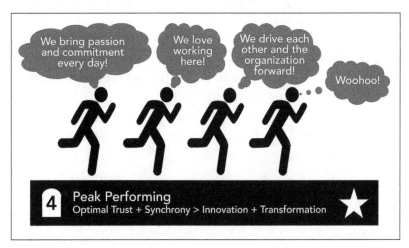

Gate 4: Peak performing

Such a group exudes psychological safety and demonstrates the qualities that Google identified in their study (empathy and turn-taking). Gate 4 teams have empathy for each other that grows from their shared trust and respect. Given that, it is natural that they seek out each other's input, because it wouldn't cross their minds not to. And, of course, they extend empathy to each other because they genuinely care about each other.

I feel fortunate to have experienced peak performance a few times in my career—or I might not believe it even exists. But it does, and it becomes the standard to which other groups are compared once you know it. When I ask people to share a time they were part of a great team, they always describe the qualities of Gate 4.

Gate 4 teams are so effective that they are a game changer for organizations, driving innovation, creativity, and productivity in ways that really move the needle on the organization's strategic goals. In fact, many organizations outsource work to other groups, even acquiring other organizations, in order to access these rare high-performing teams.

Some organizations are even experimenting with hiring intact teams that have a track record of performing well together. The group applies together and is either hired together or not at all.

In a recent "C-Suite Strategies" article in the *Wall Street Journal* titled "Companies Should Hire Teams, Not Individuals," Dr. Sydney Finkelstein of Dartmouth College describes the benefits of this unique strategy as follows:

- Avoids the impact of unconscious bias that might skew the hiring process
- Increases confidence that the team members will work well together, since they already do
- Protects against hiring individuals who overstate their skills especially in social interactions
- Ensures that the group will get up and running quickly
- Reduces the chances that in-group conflict will damage productivity

Dr. Finkelstein says, "Ultimately, hiring teams just seems intuitively right. When you're renovating a room in your house, you usually don't want to do it haphazardly, fixing only one part of the room and then making additional alterations as time passes. It's far better to think ahead, anticipate your future needs and come up with a single, unified design that will stand the test of time. Yet in companies, managers take the haphazard approach all the time. They hire individuals for different reasons and then try to cobble them together into a team afterward. All too often, it doesn't work."

So, the organization with the most Gate 4 teams has an incredible advantage over their competitors. But I would argue that instead of focusing on strategies to hire or acquire the small percentage of Gate 4 teams that exist, we should spend our energy on making sure *every* team has the support and opportunity to become a Gate 4 team.

This means leadership needs to thoughtfully form teams, ensuring that they have the safety, support, and clarity of purpose that are crucial in the early stages of their work. And we also need clear tools and interventions to use when a team is sliding off track. Fortunately, teams can be set up for success, and they can also recover or heal from early missteps. But it requires intentional effort and guidance on the part of the leaders because you must go back and fix the wrongs from the earlier gates. It absolutely can be done—I have done this with many teams—but it takes more effort than if they were supported correctly from the beginning. In section VI, I'll give you the tools to do so.

23. Journeying through the Gates

Now that we have looked at the four gates, let's explore the model as a whole. Ideally, the four gates build upon each other: a strong foundation of safety at Gate 1 creates the opportunity for more success at Gate 2. And a strong sense of purpose and sense of we becomes the precursor to a true sense of belonging. But the gates are not linear; they stack on each other, resting on what is gained or lost in the earlier levels.

Even a Gate 4 team operating at peak performance can suffer if a threat from a previous gate appears to change physical or psychological safety or clarity about the project or the resources needed to succeed. Like real gates, we should move through them in a forward progression, but if something happens, we can travel back through them as well.

The Four Gates to Peak Team Performance Model

Let's look at some examples of real teams and the potential impact of events at the various gates. For simplicity's sake, let's compare two teams (Y and Z) at the same organization, each with four members.

Members enter Gate 1 when they are pulled together to start on a new project or be part of a group. This is when they begin the largely unconscious assessment process about their safety. Gate 1 safety issues can occur during early meetings or later in the process. Consider how the following events might affect you or your team. These are real examples from current teams.

- The team leader starts a brainstorming session for the new project but actively critiques or shuts down one member's input.

- One teammate asks another teammate out on a date. After being politely declined, they continue to make advances but out of earshot of other team members or the supervisor.
- One team member overhears their teammates making a racist joke in the break room.
- In an early meeting, the team leader, who is also the supervisor, brings a baseball bat and walks around the room, smacking it into his hand as he talks about how important it is that the team hits their targets.

Any "threat" above may decrease the capacity of both individuals and the group unless actively addressed or counterbalanced by equally strong boosts. If Team Y experiences one or two of the above threats, while Team Z experiences none, Team Z will have more overall capacity and energy going in to Gate 2.

As teams enter Gate 2, they focus on purpose and assess the likelihood of succeeding at the task. Consider the impact the following real examples might have on individual team members and the group as a whole:

- The team leader is unclear about key aspects of the project and doesn't follow up with promised information/communication.
- One member has deep expertise/experience in an area but that part of the project is assigned to another teammate.
- The group has been given a nearly impossible deadline, one that would require every aspect of the project to align perfectly to meet, something that has not happened before.
- During meetings, one teammate regularly speaks over the others, taking credit for other teammates' work or implying blame for missteps on others.

These threats, if not addressed or counterbalanced by boosts, can affect the capacity of the group, with some individuals experiencing more energy loss than others. In addition, a new threat from Gate 2 can still have a strong impact. For example, if a team member experiences harassment or exclusion by the group, it can add drains here.

If both Teams Y and Z experience one threat at this gate, Team Z is still ahead on overall energy and capacity and has been able to use Gate 2 to further enhance the group's forward progress. They are likely to have a sense of we so are starting to operate as a collective and are poised for belonging and collaboration. Whereas the members of Team Y now have more reasons to be cautious about their involvement and commitment, keeping them in a state of me or, worse, moving to an us-versus-them orientation.

As you can see, going into Gate 3, Team Y would need to address their incoming deficits to have a chance of harnessing this gate's benefits. But as you can also imagine, most groups that have challenges in the first two gates rarely stop and fix what is broken.

Gate 3 is about true belonging and the teams assess key factors that help them move to an authentic sense of belonging and psychological safety, or they stall in ways that prevent peak performance. Consider how these real examples would impact teams you know:

- Teammates express their appreciation to each other for what they bring to the group. Or the opposite, teammates act disrespectfully to each other during interactions.
- People trust each other, being more authentic and vulnerable the more they engage. Or a team member breaks the trust of one or more of the group.
- The members feel safe enough to take risks and make mistakes, learning as they grow. Or people start playing it safe, hiding ideas, insights, and/or mistakes.
- When there is conflict, people address it directly and kindly. Or they engage in gossip and passive aggressive behaviors.

Gate 3 acts like a super accelerator for teams that are in good shape and Team Z is in position to see these benefits and make it to Gate 4.

As you can see, my Four Gates to Peak Team Performance model allows us to better diagnose and predict team performance. It can help team members and leaders better understand the importance of each gate and also create a call to action to set teams up for success as well as address challenges and problems quickly. Problems do not disappear on their own, they need to be intentionally and actively addressed or else their negative effects will linger, dragging the team down and preventing the group from achieving its potential or peak performance. The good news is that great teams can be created. Each gate can be maximized through specific actions that not only augment but also accelerate team safety and effectiveness. We will explore how in section VI.

Your Learning Journey

Compare two of your team experiences, one where the team succeeded and one where the team struggled or failed. Let's explore how they differed in moving through the Four Gates to Peak Team Performance. Make some notes in the table below.

	Successful Team	Struggle Team
Gate 1: Safety		
Gate 2: Purpose		
Gate 3: Belonging		
Gate 4: Peak Performing		

Comments:

STRATEGIES FOR EXECUTIVES, TEAM LEADERS & TEAM MEMBERS

"You don't inspire your teammates by showing them how amazing you are. You inspire them by showing them how amazing they are."
Robyn Benicasa, World Champion,
How Winning Works: 8 Essential Leadership Lessons from the Toughest Teams on Earth

24. Creating Gate 4 Teams

The uber-performance of Gate 4 teams doesn't just appear overnight. It develops when conditions are right, created by the combined actions of senior leaders, team leaders, and team members, and girded by some of the organization's policies. Before we give each group specific strategies, let's look at some overarching principles that apply to everyone who cares about maximizing team performance.

1. Honor the power of biology with in-person interactions.

While technology makes it possible for us to work with others through a video screen or phone, our brains were built for in-person interactions. Our brain reads meaning and intent in others through micromuscular changes in the face, body language, and pheromone signals—almost all of which is lost when we communicate through technology instead of in person. Even video conferencing loses the third dimension that can make the difference for accurately reading another's meaning.

	In Person	Video	Phone	Text/Type
Facial Expressions *Four regions of face: brow, eyes, nose, mouth*	✔	✔		
Body Language *Position, posture, lean, rapidity of movement*	✔	✔		
Vocal Intensity, pitch, intonation, pace, enunciation, silence	✔	✔	✔	
Pheromone signals	✔			
Words	✔	✔	✔	✔

In-person interactions provide the most data to the brain

When teams are in the early, trust-building stage of their time together, best practice prioritizes in-person interactions because that way all members participate using their full set of biological tools for connecting and communicating. Investing in this time together can make a huge difference in how people move through Gates 1 and 2, the foundation for success in later gates. If you can't bring people together physically, then you need to counterbalance the deficit with more frequent and in-depth interactions that intentionally fill in the gaps with helping them get to know one another and build trust.

2. Select or develop leaders whose strength is cultivating collaboration.

Effective team leadership requires emotional intelligence and collaborative intelligence—the ability to bring out the best in a group of others. Traditionally, most team leaders are selected based on their successes as individual contributors, even though that background has often been shown to actually harm the growth of a team if the person stepping into the new role doesn't know how to make that vital shift from performer to facilitator. Likewise, if you are choosing new leaders for your organization, avoid making team leaders the people who *also* supervise the team members. This time-honored strategy is a recipe for disaster because the power dynamic and performance review process make it difficult to create true psychological safety. When people know that questioning their leader might harm their future raise or promotion, they are biologically drawn to protect their personal safety (as in livelihood) first.

Instead, look for people who are already natural facilitators and amp up their team-leading abilities through training and coaching. This means looking past the star performers to the people who have rapport with lots of different people. Find the person who others are already turning to for guidance or support—the one who creates cohesion and brings out the best in others. These are the hidden gems in any organization, waiting to be tapped for leadership roles. Then make a further investment by training them on key skills and strategies.

Also be sure your performance review system evaluates team leaders based on the right set of criteria. Success should be measured against how well they create psychological safety and enhance engagement and retention, and how their teams perform on important metrics like successful task execution, collaboration, and innovation.

3. Build psychological safety.

As we have seen, psychological safety is the key differentiator for thriving teams. The way a group of people comes together and sets up to work together can either activate trust or a climate of conflict and blame. People need to learn about psychological safety and the skills they need to create and maintain it. This includes extending empathy and other facets of emotional intelligence and methods for insuring that input from each person is sought out and listened to. People need to know how to ask the kinds of questions that safely broaden and deepen the conversation. In particular, it's important for managers/leaders to learn how to counterbalance the barrier that power creates.

In her research, Harvard's Dr. Amy Edmondson found that leaders play a vital role in creating psychological safety. While the following five behaviors are part of any good leader's toolbox, team members can do them as well, sometimes counterbalancing a leader's deficit or accelerating their good leadership. Remember, on a team, leadership is everyone's job. As you read, think about how you can start using these behaviors to strengthen your teamwork.

Be accessible

Availability creates those opportunities for candor. When we rush off to the next thing, whether in person or online, we lose those informal social exchanges that can be so valuable. Consider how you might make yourself more available for small talk—knowing that there is actually nothing small about it. Managers and leaders, literally make sure your door is open so that people can just pop by. Also remember to get out of your space and go to where your team is working. "Management by walking around" is a real and effective strategy.

Acknowledge your own fallibility

Not pretending to be perfect is especially crucial for managers and leaders because it breaks down the barrier of hierarchy and builds a more authentic relationship, allowing others in turn to make their unique contribution and increasing your chance for success. Statements like "I will probably miss something so I really need your input," and "You have a different view from me—what are you seeing out there?" and "I'm not an expert in X, so I need your help" are invitations to cross the power and hierarchy divide.

Proactively invite input

Ask lots of questions to create the opening for other people to share. Edmondson recommends asking questions that broaden and deepen the conversation. Broadening questions include:

- "What do others think?"
- "What are we missing?"
- "What other options should we consider?"

Deepening questions include:
- "What's your concern?"
- "What leads you to think so?"
- "Can you give an example?"
- "What do you think might happen if we did fix X?"

While leaders and managers can and should be asking these types of questions, any member of a team can ask them.

Embrace the messengers

If you want to increase the chances that people will take risks and make mistakes, don't shoot the messenger. Leaders reacting negatively lessens the chances that people will come forward in the future. Instead, reward them for the courage it took to speak up. Say things like, "Thank you for sharing that" and "I really appreciate your input" and "I'm so grateful you brought that to my attention." This allows all the vital information and perspectives to come to the surface, where they can be addressed instead of suppressed.

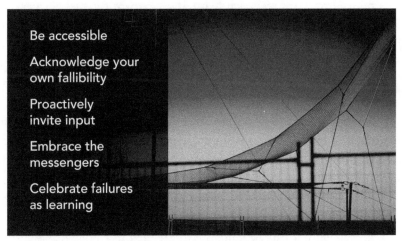

Be accessible

Acknowledge your own fallibility

Proactively invite input

Embrace the messengers

Celebrate failures as learning

Ways leaders create psychological safety

Celebrate failures as learning

Frame failures as the powerful source of information and insight that they are. Help others harvest important insights from the experience without blaming or shaming. Ask questions like, "How can we use this experience to improve?" and "What new insights did we gain?" and "What should we start doing differently today to make sure that doesn't happen again?" Some organizations even have "fail fast" or "fail forward" awards because they know that great innovation takes failure. If you don't believe me, then perhaps Grand Jedi Master Yoda will convince you, as he did Luke Skywalker in *Star Wars: The Last Jedi,* "Best learning, failure is."

But teaching psychological safety is only the beginning. It's vitally important to then watch for signs that the team is moving forward in a healthy way. If you see signs of bad norming, like increased complaints to HR, more sick days and turnover, or decreasing engagement, you must take action immediately. Otherwise, you risk creating a team paralyzed by learned helplessness, which can be very difficult to shift once it is established.

4. Invest in team training and team building.

Again, team leaders are not the only ones who create an awesome team. Members also play an important role—and they need the tools and skills to do their part, including learning the difference between team training and team building. Team training refers to the knowledge and skills needed to work well as a team and perform the task successfully, such as facility with group development, work styles, inclusion, psychological safety, communication, project management, execution, and conflict resolution, to name a few. Whereas team building is the process and interactions through which people learn about each other, both personally and professionally, as they begin building trust.

Did you know that conflict about a task correlates positively with creativity but interpersonal conflict has a negative relationship with creativity? Conflict resolution skills are vital to team health because they help the members wrestle with the diverse ideas and work styles each one brings to the team without harming the trust necessary for them to perform at their best.

To this end, it can be valuable to create a team playbook, a document that provides a centralized overview of your process to help the team navigate the combined task and relationship elements of the work. For example, it helps the team establish ground rules and guidelines, and clarifies the roles each member will play. It also becomes a tool for holding each other accountable and get back on track when and if things go wonky. Here are the essential questions and categories I recommend every good playbook include. You can download this form at www.Britt Andreatta.com/Wired-to-Connect.

Goal: Purpose: Milestones: Deadline:
Shared practices (how we work together) • Criteria for evaluating ideas • Decision-making process • Communication flow and form • Expectations for personal and interpersonal conduct • Methods for building trust and psychological safety • How and when value and effort is recognized
Roles (who does what) • Gather information • Analyze data • Coordinate efforts • Track progress • Leadership • Followership • Quality assurance • Cohesiveness and camaraderie • Other:
Resolving conflict • How and by when • Mediator • Final authority
Accountability • How measured • When assessed • Consequences
Resources • What will be provided • By whom • By when

Team building is different from training. Team building takes many forms, sometimes unfolding over regular meetings or off-site retreats. Rather than digging into the assigned task, team building is about intentionally creating experiences that build relationships, and more importantly, trust. It allows teams to put the marbles in the jar so that later, when the work gets harder, people can tussle with the challenges and still maintain psychological safety. Team building is often shortchanged in the rush to move things forward but I promise you that investing in team building on the front side will more than pay off later in the group's development and project execution.

5. Hold teams accountable as a unit.

Getting a diverse range of work styles, skills, motivations, and personalities to work together cohesively presents a set of challenges that can be made much more challenging if we inadvertently undermine people's motivation for working together by not holding them accountable as a unit. Every member of the team needs to know that they are responsible, *together,* for the successes and failures and will share equally in the rewards and consequences. This includes performance reviews and other forms of recognition and rewards. Otherwise, when things get hard, members will be tempted to focus on their own needs, which are often not aligned with what is best for the team.

As a former college professor, I can say that the academic sector learned this a long time ago. When students are asked to work in a group, they will often devolve into complaining and blaming their partners and ultimately divide the task into individual portions that they can complete without having to work together too much (i.e., cooperation). But when they know that they will receive the same grade for the product, they work much harder at communicating and collaborating because they will all suffer the fate of the outcome equally. They have skin in the game, so to speak.

The rest of the business sectors can benefit by using this strategy. Most performance processes focus on individual contributions, creating an invisible motivation for team members to prioritize their own goals and outcomes to preserve job security (think physical safety). In other words, it rests on proving their individual value, which often undermines what is best for the project, the team, and ultimately the organization.

Performance systems need to have a team component for people who work in teams, with a certain percentage of their review score based on teamwork. The best way to support teams working through differences and recovering from mistakes is to review the team as a unit and give each member the *same* team score. This fosters motivation for helping the team succeed and tangibly acknowledges the value that teamwork brings to the organization. Lack of team accountability can create a culture of blame and shame, which can cripple an organization for years.

Accountability is another reason I chose gates as the metaphor for this model. Gates swing open and shut on a hinge, with the hinge pin literally holding it all together. For teams, the hinge pin is being held accountable as a unit because it counterbalances the pull of self-protection.

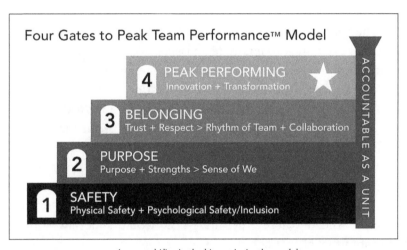

Accountability is the hinge pin in the model

There are many ways to set up this kind of performance system. Some models have leaders or supervisors assess or evaluate the team's performance, taking into account both the task as well as the collaboration or cohesiveness of the group. Another form of feedback is to have each member evaluate the group as a whole. This can be valuable because they have to address and take responsibility for their own role as well as everyone else's. Consider how you can make sure that your performance review system accurately mirrors and assesses the enormous amount of work being accomplished by teams.

25. Strategies for Senior Leaders and Executives

While team leaders directly influence a team's day-to-day effectiveness, senior leaders and executives create the broader culture and environment that either enhances or harms successful teamwork. Let's look at seven strategies you can use.

1. Make team effectiveness your #1 priority.

The research is clear: getting teams right is a real game changer for any organization. By making team effectiveness your key focus you put your energy into something that will drive huge return on investment for years to come. In organizations that are struggling or failing, leaders are sometimes more motivated to look at all possible solutions, including teams.

There's more danger for leaders in organizations that are performing well or even great to ignore team issues: when key performance and financial indicators are good, you might be tempted to think, "Why fix what ain't broke?" But studies show us that things are broken. A majority of workers are feeling the negative effects of poor teams on a daily basis. This is why I tell global leaders that their profit margin may be just fine—but wouldn't it be better if it went up 25 percent? What if the enormous costs of disengagement and turnover went down, even just 10 percent? Focusing on teams only yields improvements, and so an organization skyrockets, as author Jim Collins would say, "from good to great." And if you're great now, how would super-awesome feel? Think about what that could yield across the metrics that matter. It's a fact: organizations that focus on teams now will be the leaders in their industries well into the future, disrupting even long-established scions.

2. Assess your organization with a critical eye.

A big part of the first strategy above is being willing to look critically at your organization. You likely have lots of data that can help you assess culture and environment, but you must be willing to look for signs that people or teams are struggling. Assess the real costs to get as thorough of an understanding as you can of the current state.

For example, an engagement survey can provide a wealth of information, since the data is typically organized by manager, department, and function. Instead of looking at overall trends, dig deeper and look for signs of team health. Which groups have the lowest scores? Is this an ongoing issue or a recent dip? How does that data correlate with other things like sick days, turnover, and use/abuse of benefits and perks? Who is leaving your organization? Are women and people of color leaving faster or in greater numbers than other groups? Pay special attention to written comments in both engagement surveys and exit surveys.

Most leaders make the mistake of ignoring evidence and trends or spinning negative data to seem more positive. I once worked with a multinational company that was the global leader in its field. Their engagement data was full of waving red flags and yet I watched them congratulate themselves for being above the industry norm, despite the lowest scores in three years. Turning a blind eye to a growing problem never makes the problem go away, it just drives up the costs and increases the time it will take it fix it down the road.

Don't forget that observation is a powerful tool. Make a point of noticing who speaks in meetings and who does not. Pay attention to body language, who takes up more of the "air time," and who interrupts others. Reflect on who brings forward ideas and who gets or takes the credit. These can all be clues about the health of your organization.

3. Look at the environments that create your best teams.

This goes both ways: explore your top- and bottom-performing teams to understand how their environment operates. Teams reflect their surroundings, so by looking at what differentiates the successful from the struggling you will discover what should be replicated and what must be fixed. Also look for the drains and boosters in play to measure the impact they are having on teams' ability to move through the gates.

Remember, Google's study found that top-performing teams were not made of the top-performing people, but rather grew out of groups that created psychological safety. Psych safety will play a role in your organization too, but now you can discover how people are creating it so you can replicate that across all the functions. Shine the light on what's working and acknowledge those who are doing a great job. Recognition matters and whatever you reward you will get more of.

You will also inevitably discover areas that will and should bother you. Places where people feel threatened or unsafe and management or leadership styles that range from neglect to open hostility. You may find evidence of harassment, bullying, and aggression. While difficult to see, these areas need to be identified and addressed as soon as possible if you want an organization where teams and people thrive.

So don't wait to take action. The longer a divisive person stays in their role or a dysfunctional group stays on that same trajectory, the more energy is draining away every day and the more likely learned helplessness will take hold.

This offers you a great opportunity to show your organization that you mean what you say about creating a great culture. Michele Mollkoy, a learning executive at a major hospital says, "What you permit, you promote." Whatever you discover is already known to the people who see it and live it every day. Once you see it, they will be watching you to see if you are going to fix it or collude with it by turning your back.

This also means that you need to hold leaders accountable for the performance of their teams and people. Leaders and managers should have their own set of performance criteria that include how well they create psychological safety, promote or enhance engagement, and build environments where people can collaborate and innovate. When they know they are responsible and accountable for the health of their team, they will make it their focus. This is the fastest way to shift the culture in your organization.

Case Study: Global Consulting Firm
Org Size: Large

"For the majority of my time at my firm, I have worked on projects with the same team leader. I met her by happenstance and luck, but because she was such a great leader/manager I have stuck with her ever since. Consulting firms are interesting because you change teams and work with lots of different people. Every time you work with someone, it creates almost like a digital credential, and every time you ask to join another project, some-one asks for that credential to make sure you're a fit.

Furthermore, when people are joining projects, they always want to know if the leader they are working for has positive or negative credentials, and will often ask around. This woman has amazing credentials, and like a magnet, she attracts good talent. What's most impressive is that not only does she attract high

---

138 | BRITT ANDREATTA

performers, but in my opinion, she also attracts good-natured people, which is seen through the types of people that work on her team, and their own characteristics as well as how they engage with others.

For me, what makes her so great is that she creates a sense of psychological safety for all of us who work for her, very much like what Google studied and found with Project Aristotle. It fits it to a tee. She empowers us to think and act like owners and to strive for more, which allows all of us to go above and beyond what we think we are capable of because we feel supported and empowered to do so. Sometimes we fail or fall down, and she supports us 100 percent through those moments, which also gives us the confidence to keep swinging and taking risks.

This has yielded several great outcomes. Her teams have accomplished several successful projects with positive feedback from clients. The organization benefits with repeat business from those clients (often with even bigger contracts) as well as referrals to new business. And this leader was promoted to Managing Director much quicker than the average Senior Manager. She also has assumed responsibility for a number of programs and initiatives that very few people at her level have.

We need more leaders who emulate her genuine effort to motivate, care, and inspire her team and know how to create an environment of radical candor and psychological safety."

4. Pivot from performer to facilitator.

Senior leaders and executives need to also consider themselves facilitators. The functions or departments that report to you are all teams of a sort, and your direct reports are a kind of team as well. Your role is to facilitate them, using collaborative intelligence to create the environment that brings out *their* best performance.

To be a real leader you cannot rest on the laurels of your position or status. Dig into your own development; be willing to learn and grow. I recommend focusing on developing emotional intelligence, empathy, and collaborative intelligence, with a special focus on psychological safety.

Model the qualities that create psychological safety for your team: Be accessible. Acknowledge your own fallibility. Proactively invite input through questions that broaden and deepen the discussion. Embrace the messengers. Celebrate failures as learning. Giving your group the important opportunity to watch you create psychological safety and also experience it themselves allows them to then model their behavior after yours and replicate that with their groups.

I believe every leader can learn these skills, though some struggle and some may not have the ability to authentically create safety for others or facilitate the best environment without work or intervention. It's okay if this is true for you, just be sure to surround yourself with people who are great at it as a counterbalance, while you focus on your strengths. Don't ignore this vital element; delegate it to others who excel, to ensure your people and organization get what they need.

5. Invest in great learning.

Learning is the way all humans grow and improve. In today's fast-moving world, five years is the half-life of any learned skill, which means that professional development is now an integral part of our careers. Smart leaders know that to keep an organization at the front of its field, its people must continually hone their knowledge and skills.

Investing in great learning is different from offering training programs. Neuroscience has shed light on how people learn new things and shift their behavior (read more in my book *Wired to Grow*) and technology has given us many more tools for designing and delivering great learning experiences. If you have not already focused on creating a culture of learning, you should. Here are some compelling reasons:

- Top-performing organizations are five times more likely to have a learning culture than lower-performing ones.
- Learning culture accounts for 46 percent of overall improved business outcomes including innovation, time to market, and market share.
- Every 10 percent increase in learning effectiveness increases employee engagement by 4 percent.
- Employees spend 40 percent of their time at work learning.
- "Ability to learn and progress" is one of the biggest differentiators for Millennials when choosing a place to work. In fact, 42 percent say they will likely leave their organization because they are not learning fast enough.

Investing in learning is not just about offering more workshops. It's about creating a culture that promotes and supports continuous improvement. Hire experienced learning professionals who can implement the right solutions at the right times and who know how to leverage current and cutting-edge options for maximum effectiveness. Learning offers a great return on investment (ROI), so every dollar you put in will pay for itself and then some. For example, emotional intelligence training has been shown to have an ROI as high as 1,000 percent!

As good learning uplevels the performance of your people and teams, it also contributes to your employee brand, helping attract and retain better talent. The right learning experiences can also act as boosters that mitigate or counterbalance the negative effect of drains. For example, organizations are now offering mindfulness programs and reaping rewards in employee performance and lowered health costs.

1. Make teams your #1 priority

2. Assess with a critical eye

3. Look at the environments that create your best teams

4. Pivot from performer to facilitator

5. Invest in great learning

6. Hire a talent management leader

7. Protect your peak-performing teams

Strategies for senior leaders and executives

6. Hire a talent-management leader to sit above HR.

What's the difference between human resource and talent-management professionals? Human resource professionals tend to hold a risk-mitigation perspective that focuses on the transactional aspects of employment, like compensation and benefits, payroll, and training, where they often are focused on containing the impact of the poorest performers or the "lowest-common denominator." Talent management professionals take a more holistic view, looking at what supports the organization's strategic growth and development, including how to bring out the best in people and teams.

Traditionally, HR folks are brought on early in an organization's development to handle the setup of key systems. But, eventually, organizations do best when a senior talent-management person is hired to direct an organization's people and culture. If you have not already made this important shift, do so now. The talent management leader should be part of the executive team, a peer to the other senior roles, reporting to the CEO. I also recommend that various function heads (HR, talent acquisition, learning, etc.), are given equal titles and roles, and that all report to the talent-management leader. Learning housed under HR tends to prioritize training and risk mitigation, rather than creating a true culture of learning and improvement.

Again, make sure that your entire performance review process aligns with recognizing and rewarding the behaviors that drive real success. This includes adding team elements to your assessment process, and holding managers and leaders accountable for their groups' health, performance, and growth. Make learning and progress part of your evaluation process. A senior talent-management professional can easily implement these initiatives plus many more that will help your organization reach new levels of success.

7. Protect your peak-performing teams.

Finally, do all that you can to protect your Gate 4 teams. As we now know, achieving Gate 4 performance is rare, so when it happens don't mess it up. Keep the group together. Protect them from unnecessary reorganizations and changes in leadership. Keep them in the high-performance flow as long as you can. And don't waste their Gate 4 level on less demanding tasks. Make sure they are doing the innovative and collaborative work and leave the cooperation and coordination to the teams still moving through the early gates.

These strategies will help you grow more and more Gate 4 teams. Eventually you will be more fluid, with the entire organization supporting team success and excellence. Until then, be mindful of protecting and supporting your high-performing teams currently in play.

26. Strategies for Team Leaders and Managers

Leaders have the most critical role in the team ecosystem. Your words and actions directly influence the day-to-day effectiveness of your team as well as how much your team fulfills its full potential. But no pressure!

This may seem intimidating, but there are several simple, effective strategies you can use for guidance. Your biggest challenge is just making sure you spend enough time and energy on them. To help you, start strategies before the team even comes together so that you can launch in the best way possible.

Before a Team Convenes

Resist the temptation to start leading only at the first meeting. Your role starts the second you know you will be leading a team. This critical time period can make the difference between a great launch and a failed one.

Make the pivot from performer to facilitator. Your role is now about creating an environment where this group of people can thrive. It should no longer be about your ideas and contributions to the project but rather helping your team leverage theirs. Some people find this a difficult switch to make, especially if you have done well as a performer. To counterbalance that natural urge, focus on developing collaborative intelligence skills. (I recommend reading the books *The Collaboration Instinct* and *Collaborative Intelligence*.)

Also develop your skills as a coach. Coaching is different from directing. By learning more about coaching you will gain a useful set of tools, questions, and processes that naturally help others thrive. I have found that team leaders are better at holding back their urge to direct when they can channel that focus into coaching. Lisa Gates has a great online course for honing coaching skills on LinkedIn Learning. I also recommend the MMS Institute and the book *Transformational Life Coaching* by its cofounder Cherie Carter-Scott, recognized as the "mother of coaching." (I earned my own coaching certificate with MMS and I think it's the best in the world.)

Before you call your first team meeting, create your plan for helping them successfully move through the four gates. Don't just wing it. The stakes are too high to hope it all turns out okay. Think through how you can maximize in-person time together. If you can't, then counterbalance with more in-depth interactions online. Look for ways to enhance those all-important early interactions so your new team starts building trust and psychological safety.

Also learn what you can about your group in advance. What are their strengths and areas of expertise? What experiences have they already had on teams in your organization? What do you know about their professional and personal purpose? You want to role model being inclusive and teach your team how to create an inclusive environment. Dr. Christine Cox states, "If we're not actively including, we're accidentally excluding."

Learn what resources are available to your team in terms of learning experiences, support, and processes for resolving conflict or dealing with inappropriate behavior. Do your homework and, if you are unsure, check in with the appropriate people so you are clear on the project, purpose, and resources. Your team's work depends on your ability to effectively communicate these critical items.

First Gate: Safety

Now let's explore some strategies specific to each gate. As the team convenes, remember that the first gate sows the seeds of safety and trust. So be very attentive to the group, regularly taking the temperature to see how it is doing in these areas:

1. Be intentional about how you launch the team.
Take the time to plan your agenda so that you can leverage everything that will help your team excel. Have people meet in person. Focus equally on the task or project and on building relationships. Plan appropriate ice breakers that help people get to know each other in nonthreatening ways.

2. Offer your people team training and team building.
Teach your group about the four gates and give them tools to be great at teaming. Provide them with training on team skills and opportunities for team building. As stated, I prioritize group development, work styles (like the Five Dynamics model), psychological safety, inclusion, communication, project management and execution, and conflict resolution. Your learning department likely has some helpful resources, so reach out early to get the most out of the tools at your disposal.

3. Immediately address issues that threaten safety.

If you see signs of bullying, harassment, or aggression, address them immediately and firmly. By taking the issue seriously, you send an important signal about prioritizing safety. This can go a long way to repair damage done by an insensitive or hurtful person, as it can be doubly painful to feel threatened or invalidated and then have a leader take no action—essentially condoning the behavior. A team may likely recover from a problematic coworker but not from a leader who turns their back.

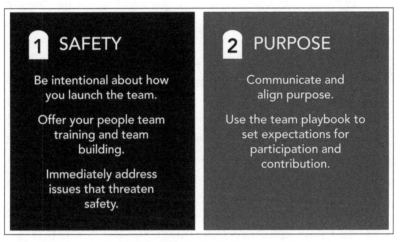

Strategies for team leaders in Gates 1 and 2

Second Gate: Purpose

Team leaders play an important role in the second gate, providing critical information to the team on the task and its purpose.

1. Communicate and align purpose.

As the leader, you will likely be the person informing the team of the project or task. Be sure to frame it as it relates to the organization's primary purpose. If you struggle to do so, you're team will likely struggle to see the connection as well. Work with leaders above you to craft a clear vision and project statement that you can articulate easily and consistently. Further, your team will excel if you can connect the project to each of their individual purposes.

Case Study: Staffing Business Service
Org Size: Medium

"When I was new to my current organization, I inherited a team of individuals who were all located in different offices, who hadn't worked together before, and were all new to their roles. My reception was mixed as some weren't welcoming of an outsider, some were ambivalent, and others were excited about the prior experience I brought to the team.

There are three key factors that brought this team to a high level of performance. There were three keys to success in bringing this team together.

Aligning them around one unifying vision, something that was bigger than each of them yet they could claim a big stake in its success. We chose placing in *Training* magazine's 'Training Top 125' list. All of our actions were aligned around achieving that one vision, which we accomplished within our goal of two years. Even in the first year, when we knew we wouldn't place, a member of the team encouraged (almost forced) us to apply so we could go through the experience together with no expectation of placing.

As all team members were located in different offices, it was essential to our team development that we came together on a quarterly basis in the first year and half to create shared experiences for the team to increase bonding and fully develop intrateam relationships. As the team leader, I was very intentional in ensuring we created team bonding experiences, which were inclusive to each member's preferences, and respected each member as an individual. For example, we rotated locations for our in-person meetings rather than having everyone come to HQ. When we were together in anyone's home city, we would go out to an event that they would normally do themselves so that we could learn to understand each other in a context outside of work. We also had dinners together, getting to know each other on a more personal level.

Each team member was assigned a specialty area of responsibility. This way, no one was competing for work, yet felt that they were all complimentary to each other. They would individually consult each other regarding their area of specialty and respected each position they held.

There were two key outcomes. First, we achieved our goal of being in the Training Top 125. The team went together to celebrate this victory at the awards gala and celebrated two years of hard work. The second outcome I noticed is that while in the beginning I was very much out front of the team as the leader, with them all coming to me for advice, I have eventually moved to a supportive role behind them. Now, they all consult each other rather than only looking to me for advice or decisions. Our team meetings are not led by me, but are facilitated by the group and led by the jointly agreed-upon agenda."

2. Use the team playbook to set expectations for participation and contribution.
A team playbook is a great tool to use to help the team get clear about the goal, milestones, communication, roles, and the process for conflict resolution. You don't have to decide these elements yourself but rather facilitate the team in discussing and agreeing to the various elements. Later, you can remind them as needed of what they agreed to and hold them accountable. Use the playbook described in chapter 24.

3. Continually advocate for your team.
Your role as team leader is to set your team up to succeed. Be sure your team has what they need to accomplish what is being asked of them. This means clearing barriers or roadblocks and encouraging and advocating for your members. If you need to, communicate questions up the hierarchy, passing on concerns or requests.

Third Gate: Belonging

Your team will either accelerate or struggle at this gate, depending on how they have come through Gates 1 and 2. If they are not in good shape, slow down, and resolve issues that are brewing. While you may feel "behind," resist the urge to add more pressure as this will likely exacerbate the problems. Go back and fix what is not working. If you are not sure how, seek help from your supervisor or another appropriate leader. Then use these strategies to move your team forward.

1. Recognize value, effort, and progress.

As we have learned, people have an innate need to feel part of a group and to contribute value. To ensure your team knows their efforts are appreciated, design a process for recognition that's easy to implement. And make sure it's not forgotten or pushed aside when things get busy. To be fair and consistent, use your calendar or other organization systems to help you track team members and deliver frequent feedback.

Also ask the group to create their own method for recognizing each other. Kudos from the leader are nice, but can be even more effective when they come from peers. As you help the group work through the team playbook, be sure you have them home in on acknowledgment practices to reinforce each other's value, effort, and progress.

2. See the mirror your team reflects back.

Here's what I have learned from my years of consulting and researching: teams act like a mirror, reflecting back to the people who lead them. When your team excels, it's mirroring the kind of guidance you provide. That's usually something team leaders embrace, but when a team is failing or struggling, it can be uncomfortable for a leader to see their own ineffective leadership. However, it's actually a great gift if you can learn to see it as one. It's amazing feedback that gives clues about what needs to shift in your leadership.

For example, if your team is being critical of each other, ask yourself where you're being critical in your life. Don't limit your reflection to the team itself as it make be reflecting another area of your life at work or at home (not necessarily with the team although that can be true too). If your team is not feeling safe enough to take risks, it's likely that you don't feel safe enough to take risks in some other area of your life. What is true about mirrors is that once you resolve the challenge in your own life, your team will likely shift too, continuing the mirror-like effect. If you need support, consider partnering up with a coach or mentor—someone you trust—and talking it through.

3. Empower your team to resolve conflict.

Conflict is an inevitable part of group development and collaborative work so it's going to happen on your team. Therefore, make sure you and your team are prepared with an agreed-upon process before issues arise. For example, it's common for people to get in the habit of always taking their grievances to the team leader, instead of resolving things themselves. Encourage your team to resolve issues in a mature and respectful way, so that you are not always refereeing their interactions.

I strongly recommend the following:

- Help the group establish a mature, respectful default process for handling friction and differences of opinion. For example, they have a one-on-one conversation using tools they learned during training for having difficult conversations or they have an open forum with the other team members weighing in on the issue.

- If they are not able to resolve the issue themselves, then they can come to you...together. In this meeting, they must share what they have already tried and why they are stuck. This piece is the game changer because it keeps you from getting pulled into a negative vortex of whining, or "tattling" sessions where you only get one side of the story.

- After hearing all the information, you provide guidance on how to resolve the issue and make the final decision. (Note: For serious issues of bullying or harassment, immediately follow your organization's policies and procedures.)

This kind of process delineates your role as the mediator or final authority, and it sets an important expectation that your team must be able to have frank conversations with each other and hold each other accountable. Those skills will accelerate your group's ability to perform.

A lot of teams hang out in Gate 3 for a while. That's okay, as long as you are attending to the group's needs and they seem to be in a positive and healthy place with each other. Sometimes they just need a little time to settle in to their groove.

But if the group stalls out in Gate 3, doing well but not great, it's likely that there are some unspoken or unresolved issues that are keeping them from dropping into authentic belonging and trust. Sadly, that will keep the group locked here, unable to move forward until things are handled. Fortunately, Gate 3 teams can often be unstuck when leaders help them have some difficult and authentic conversations. If you don't feel comfortable facilitating this process yourself, bring in someone who does. I personally have done this work with several teams and it's amazing how much things can shift in as little as one day.

Sometimes, however, too much damage occurred at earlier stages, or the group has moved into learned helplessness, and are not willing to try and build trust or take any more risks. In this case, you may just have to hold them together as best you can, knowing that you will not likely get the highest performance out of them.

The good news is that teams that excel in Gate 3 can now move on to the rare but wonderful Gate 4 level of peak performance.

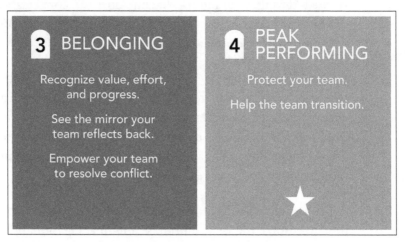

Strategies for team leaders in Gates 3 and 4

Fourth Gate: Peak Performing

While Gate 4 teams are rare, they can actually be created by how you lead them. By understanding brain science and using the Four Gates to Peak Team Performance model, you can create an environment where teams thrive. But once a team hits Gate 4, don't lean back and relax. Your job now is to help them stay there as long as possible.

1. Protect your team.
A Gate 4 team is like a receiver in football who has caught the ball and is running toward the end zone. You want to do everything in your power to clear their path and keep anyone or anything from knocking them down. The only way others will know your team has hit the rare state of peak performance is if you talk about how well your team is doing. This is vital for others to know so they can also participate in protecting the team.

Stay alert to organizational shifts that could impact your team, like possible reorganization or changes in project priorities. Speak up and advocate for them in order to create more time for them to stay in the peak-performance zone. Also be mindful of hiring plans, as the addition of a new member will drastically shift the dynamic. If you are thinking about leaving, consider your timing too as your announcement and departure will impact the team.

2. Help the team transition.

Even when you do a great job at protecting your team, its run will eventually come to an end. It's inevitable, with all the change that occurs in today's organizations. When things shift, continue to lead by helping team members transition to their new status. Take the time to celebrate together, reflecting on what you accomplished and harvesting important lessons from the experience. This is an important but often forgotten practice, so make it a hallmark of your leadership.

As your people move to new teams or projects, remind them of the Four Gates to Peak Team Performance model so they understand that they need to start the process again, now with their newfound teaming skills and experience. This is especially true if several members will still be together because they'll likely try to pick up where they left off, which can be alienating for new members.

You have the power to build Gate 4 teams. If you put the time and energy into management, honing your skills and using these strategies, you will see the impact of your leadership on your groups and your organization.

27. Strategies for Team Members

Most of us will be members of teams numerous times throughout our professional and personal lives. So it's vitally important that we all know how to create our own best experience, to drive our own success and well-being in a group setting. Here are some strategies to use at each of the four gates.

First Gate: Safety

A team's successful start determines its ultimate outcomes and the well-being of its members. In an ideal world you would have competent senior and team leaders who know how to set your group up for success. Until then, be an active participant and approach the launch of your team with attention and intention. Even if you are new to the organization or junior to the other members, you can make significant contributions and exert influence by asking good questions, offering suggestions, and modeling the right actions. Here are some things to focus on.

1. Be intentional about how you start on a team.
Join with an open mind. Focus on understanding the task and building rapport among group members. Take time to get to know people, asking questions about their lives and sharing information about yours. Linger after meetings to chat casually and take advantage of (or suggest) opportunities to have coffee. Interactions like these give your brain vital information about how to relate to and engage with each other. Be conscious of including all team members and not accidentally excluding someone, even if they appear to be distancing themselves.

2. Be mindful of building trust and psychological safety.
The roots of trust and psychological safety start now. As you see the importance of early interactions first-hand, you will likely do a better job of showing up and doing your part, as well as assessing things accurately.

    This goes both ways: you assess how safe you feel and how much trust to extend, while others are assessing how much safety and trust they feel with you. For yourself, be more intentional about gathering information so you can make accurate assessments. Pay attention to what people say and do, and be willing to ask questions instead of making assumptions. It's better to confirm an impression than be wrong later.

Be aware that your words and actions have an impact on others. Think about how you create psychological safety for others and how you earn their trust. These moments are easily harmed by unintentional insensitivity that does more damage than many people realize. I recommend that you dial up your awareness of many aspects of people's identities, from gender and race to sexual orientation and spirituality. Many organizations are now switching from diversity training to focusing on inclusion. Take advantage of these opportunities to learn and improve your cultural competence. LinkedIn Learning has several great online courses; I recommend *Unconscious Bias* by Stacey Gordon, and Pat Wadors's course *Diversity, Inclusion, and Belonging*. The following collection of TED talks also gives a well-rounded overview:

- *Inclusion, Exclusion, Illusion, and Collusion* by Dr. Helen Turnbull
- *The Danger of a Single Story* by Chimamanda Ngozi Adichie
- *Cultural Difference in Business* by Valerie Hoeks
- *Did You Hear the One About the Iranian-American?* by Maz Jobrani
- *The Paradox of Diversity* by Dr. Marilyn Sanders Mobley

I strongly recommend the book *Privilege, Power, and Difference* by Allan Johnson. I learned a lot from it and have returned to it many times for guidance and insight. Vernā Myers's book *Moving Diversity Forward: Move from Well-Meaning to Well-Doing* is good as is Jennifer Brown's book *Inclusion: Diversity, The New Workplace and the Will to Change*.

As noted, the early weeks in a team are crucial for building safety and trust. It does not happen overnight and it can easily be harmed. So give team building the attention and care it deserves and you will create a strong foundation that will catapult the team's later efforts forward in big ways.

3. Immediately address issues of safety.
As you engage with your team, address problems that arise as quickly as you can. Teams and people suffer the most harm when issues drag on. This applies to everything from the tactical elements of executing the project to interpersonal relationships that threaten psychological safety and trust.

Remember, in this gate our brains are sorting for our physical and emotional safety, so home in on any potential physical and/or verbal aggression, bullying, harassment, career harm, or exclusion. Write down what happened to start your documentation and talk it over with a trusted friend outside of work. Your first priority should be feeling safe, whether addressing the problem or person directly, seeking advice from your manager or team leader, speaking with human resources, and/or seeking legal counsel.

If you are tempted to think, "This will get better," or "I don't want to be seen as a trouble maker," remember that your biology is now on alert. And if the person already exhibited behaviors that made you feel unsafe, they are likely to continue without some kind of new awareness and intentional behavior change on their part.

Speaking up means asking questions in the group, stating how you feel or what you want, and/or speaking privately with a team leader, manager, or someone in HR. It all depends on the nature of the issue and how much trust and safety has been established.

Speaking up can be for ourselves as well as on behalf of others. It can be difficult to know what to do when you see someone else being treated in a way that seems inappropriate. You might be thinking, "Should I let them handle it themselves?" or "If they aren't saying anything, maybe it's not a problem." But often, people are in the fight-flight-freeze response triggered by what happened and/or they don't feel safe enough to say or do something. Speaking up means you are taking responsibility for the good of the team, and it can often play a critical role in shifting things.

This kind of conversation can be hard, so prepare yourself beforehand. I recommend reading books like *Fierce Conversations* or *Crucial Conversations* or taking my online training on having difficult conversations (learn more at www.BrittAndreatta.com/training). Practice with a friend so you begin building the neural pathways that will help you feel ready and be more successful in achieving the goal of your communication.

Second Gate: Purpose

Since this gate is about purpose and contribution, you will want to be proactive in getting the information you need to accurately assess your situation. Remember, the goal is to replace some of your brain's automatic and unconscious assessments so you can be more intentional about the process. The strategies below will help.

1. Gather information and ask questions.
Hopefully, your team leader will bring you clear information about the project purpose and how it aligns with the organization's mission, vision, and values. If not, don't let that get in your way. Ask questions about the task, the milestones, and the resources so you can accurately assess the project and how you can best contribute and succeed.

Bring the team playbook handout (chapter 24) with you and suggest that your group use it. Whether they do or not, you can use it as a guide for questions to ask the group and leader.

As you interact with team members, be sure to use the strategies for creating psychological safety outlined in chapter 24. Ask questions that broaden and deepen the conversation. Extend empathy to others and be intentional about seeking input from every member. This means invite everyone to contribute and specifically ask for each person's thoughts or reactions. Otherwise, the people who are comfortable talking in a group will take up the airtime and it will feel like you had a productive conversation when you actually only got input from 20 percent of the team. Asking each person to comment, in the meeting or through an online process, ensures that all input is available to help the team succeed.

2. Know your own strengths and purpose.
You will enhance your ability to contribute to the group if you are familiar with and confident in your strengths. Most professionals gain this knowledge with time and experience but you can support that process by taking an appropriate assessment. Three of my favorites are the Strengths Finder, the Five Dynamics, and the Leadership Practices Inventory. All have affiliated books and workshops; learn more by searching online.

You should also get clarity about your purpose and pay attention to what is meaningful to you. Some people are quite clear about their purpose from as early as childhood, while many of us have to explore and revise as we move through life. I highly recommend the Purpose Profile offered by Imperative and the accompanying book by Aaron Hurt, *The Purpose Economy*. I also recommend *Finding Your Element* by Ken Robinson, *Essentialism* by Greg McKeown, *A Life at Work* by Thomas

Moore, *Let Your Life Speak* by Parker Palmer, and *Sacred Contracts* by Caroline Myss.

3. Be your own CEO (chief energy officer).
As you interact with your team, notice what drains your energy or capacity and what boosts it. Often, just tuning into this biological process can help us learn valuable things about ourselves and what helps us thrive. Pay attention and do your best to minimize the drains and maximize the boosts.

While we cannot always control our work environments or our colleagues, we all have the power to take better care of ourselves. Spend time with people with whom you feel safe. Focus on the meaningful aspects of the project or organization that matter to you. Use self-care practices like mindfulness to give yourself strength. This doesn't mean ignoring bad conditions (they need to be addressed) but it does mean that you do your best to manage the impact it has, helping yourself thrive in all the ways that you can.

If you notice that you and others on your team are not doing well, be proactive and talk to someone. It is much better to pause now and try to fix the problems rather than push forward and hope things will get better. The group will not be able to succeed unless safety and purpose issues are addressed.

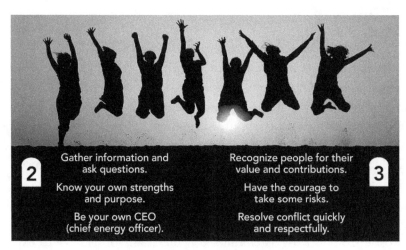

Strategies for team members in Gates 2 and 3

Third Gate: Belonging

By the time you enter this third gate, you and your team should have enough safety and clarity of purpose in place that you can really start to focus on performance. Here are strategies to maximize your success at this stage:

1. Recognize people for their value and contributions.
Knowing that we bring value is a large part of how our brain assesses belonging. So aid others by communicating your appreciation for what they bring to the group, thereby also creating the opening for them to do the same for you.

This doesn't mean offering shallow platitudes but rather authentic comments about what you value. You don't have to be close friends with someone or even like them personally to value their contribution to the project or team. Most of us are so busy that we don't take the time to recognize others. Doing so will help your team move forward and contribute to enhanced belonging.

2. Have the courage to take some risks.
The work you have been doing to build psychological safety and trust creates the safety net that allows you and your teammates to take risks. Taking risks is vulnerable and requires some courage but now is the time to start building and using your safety net.

Start small and, as you gain confidence in the safety net and your team, push yourself and others. True innovation and collaboration require both taking risks and making mistakes so you want to be mindful that every group interaction supports that. Once one person goes first, the rest are likely to follow, shifting the entire dynamic. Hopefully your team leader is guiding this process but if not, you can still maximize the success of your group by modeling it for others.

3. Resolve conflict quickly and respectfully.
Conflict is an inevitable part of teamwork but it is something most people find challenging once it arises. Not many people are comfortable with conflict, which is why it's so important to put an agreed-upon process in place before an issue arises. The team playbook outlined in chapter 24 has a section on conflict, and I always recommend creating this crucial process before it's needed. That way, it's neutral and uninfluenced by the people or project involved.

Do your part to use the conflict resolution process you've outlined, addressing things as soon as you can. Resist the urge to gossip and do not participate if people try to gossip with you. Maintaining respect for your colleagues during a time of conflict only enhances trust and psychological safety. Mishandling or not addressing conflict can quickly erode them. Make sure you and your teammates spend sufficient time detailing your conflict process and then use it consistently throughout the project. Remember, respecting someone doesn't mean you have to agree with them. Heated debates are often crucial to innovation and success. It's *how* you go about it that matters.

Fourth Gate: Peak Performing

At this point, your team is operating like a well-oiled machine, so keep doing what you are doing! Continue to create psychological safety, take risks, value each other's contributions, and resolve conflicts quickly and respectfully. You can enjoy the efficiency that Gate 4 brings as you easily drop into synchrony and don't need as much formal communication to operate at your top level. In this gate, the following strategies will extend your time in peak performance:

1. Protect your rare status.
The bigger focus now should be on protecting your group from anything that could threaten the effectiveness of the team or its members. Don't take this window of peak productivity for granted. It's a rare thing and something will eventually shift, so you want to take advantage of this time to be as productive as possible. Make sure you use your time on a Gate 4 team to focus on the most important priorities, especially those that involve collaboration and innovation.

2. Celebrate your successes.
One of the joys of being part of a Gate 4 team is the success you will have along the way. The reward centers of the brain really love recognition for a job well done, whether it's a simple high five or an elaborate celebration. Take time to celebrate successes and spend time enjoying the camaraderie of your teammates. This can further enhance belonging and create a booster for even higher levels of performance.

3. When things shift, be intentional about rebuilding the team.

No matter how great things are, organizational growth or change will ultimately shift something in your group. Perhaps a member will leave or a new member comes onboard. Maybe your team leader or a senior leader changes. Maybe the project or priorities shift. No matter the source, don't just keep trying to operate at Gate 4. Intentionally take yourself back through the gates, rebuilding safety, purpose, and belonging as you go.

Underestimating the impact that a change in even one member can have is a common mistake in team management. They erroneously think that since most of the group is intact, they can either bring the new person up to speed or work around him or her. Both options will ultimately undermine a team as they can harm the building of safety and trust that everything else rests on. Worse, it can make the new member feel excluded, which is hard to recover from once it happens. So take the time to intentionally build this new team from Gate 1. You may be able to move through the gates more quickly than you did before, but you cannot bypass them.

Together, the strategies for all four gates empower you to take an active role in your team's development and performance. Like any skill, you will get better with practice so start doing them today.

28. Conclusion: Final Thoughts on Teams

> ## Case Study: Technology
> *Org size: Large*
>
> "We were given a seemingly impossible task—organizing hundreds of subject matter experts and stakeholders to build an onboarding curriculum for new employees. We all loved the process as well as the outcome! Not only did we deliver but the stakeholders and SMEs reportedly loved working with us as cocreators throughout the project. I believe our great performance was rooted in strong leadership, common values, shared approach, equal 'skin in the game,' complementary skill sets, and some kind of intangible I've never seen before. I bet this book would help me uncover the real 'why' but that team was the best I've ever been a part of. It was magic!"

It's clear that teams drive much of the world's economy, both today and well into the future. As a result, we will likely be part of both professional and personal teams for the duration of our lives. By leveraging new insights from neuroscience, scholarly research, and internal assessment, we can approach team development in new and more effective ways.

My hope is that the Four Gates to Peak Team Performance model gives you a better understanding of how to create and recreate high-performing teams in all kinds of settings. Teams can be the source of some of our greatest experiences and accomplishments, driving belonging and ultimately happiness or even joy.

In your hands, you hold the key to the difference between a great team and a mediocre or poor one. We all have the ability to build teams that thrive and succeed so begin today by implementing the model and its corresponding strategies. Even better, convene a team that will help you expand the practices across your organization.

This model is now the centerpiece for team training at organizations in every industry. It is helping leaders around the world design and implement better team experiences. Learn more at www.Britt Andreatta.com/Wired-to-Connect or at www.7thMindInc.com. You'll also find information there about my research on change and the Change Quest™ model.

I'll close by saying that we all have the ability to fulfill our potential and to help those around us do the same. I find brain science to be a particularly helpful tool for bringing out the best in people and organizations. I encourage you to continue learning and growing—that's what this life is all about. And the more we do it together, the more we can change the world.

Thank you for taking this learning journey with me.

Warmly,

Synthesize Your Learning Journey into Action

As we conclude, look over your notes from the various learning journeys in this book. You should now have a robust understanding of teams and how to set them up for success. Take a moment to finalize your notes and create an action plan that will unfold over the next few weeks and months.

- What are your three biggest takeaways from this book?
- What are some actions you can take in the next 30, 60, and 90 days that will help you thrive as a team member?
- If you are in the role of team leader or executive, what are some actions you can take in the next 30, 60, and 90 days that will uplevel team or organization?
- Consider how you might share some of what you have learned with colleagues and leaders in your organization. For additional resources and training materials to help you, visit www.BrittAndreatta.com or www.7thMindInc.com.

REFERENCES

INTRODUCTION

Law, V. (1960). *Daily Review.* Retrieved from https://www.knowyourphrase. com/there-s-no-i-in-team

Andreatta, B. (2015). *Wired to grow: Harness to the power of brain science to master any skill.* Santa Barbara, CA: 7th Mind Publishing.

I: THE POWER OF TEAMS TODAY

Lencioni, P. (2002). *The five dysfunctions of a team: A leadership fable.* San Francisco, CA: Jossey-Bass.

Chapter 1

The Ken Blanchard Companies. (n.d.). *Annual survey.* Retrieved from http:// www.kenblanchard.com/img/pub/pdf_critical_role_teams.pdf

Center for Creative Leadership. (2015, October). *The state of teams.* Retrieved from https://www.ccl.org/wp-content/uploads/2015/04/StateOf Teams.pdf

Bersin, J. (2016, May). Global Human Capital Trends 2016. *Deloitte University Press.* Retrieved from https://www2.deloitte.com/content/dam/ Deloitte/global/Documents/HumanCapital/gx-dup-global-human-capital-trends-2016.pdf

Bersin, J. (2016). Predictions for 2016: A bold new world of talent learning, leadership, and HR technology ahead. *Deloitte University Press.* Retrieved from https://www2.deloitte.com/content/dam/Deloitte/at/ Documents/human-capital/bersin-predictions-2016.pdf

Chapter 2

Gordon, K. (n.d.). *The organizational team dynamics survey. The 5 Dynamics.* Retrieved from https://www.5dynamics.com/resource/hrd-series-1-creating-happier-healthier-employees

Gallup. (2017). *State of the global workplace.* Retrieved from http://news.gallup. com/reports/220313/state-global-workplace-2017.aspx

Society for Human Resource Management (SHRM). (n.d.). *Placing dollar costs on turnover.* Retrieved from https://www.shrm.org/resourcesandtools/ hr-topics/behavioral-competencies/critical-evaluation/pages/placing-dollar-costs-on-turnover.aspx

Budzier, A., & Flyvbjerg, B. (2011, September). Why your IT may be riskier than you think. *Harvard Business Review.* Retrieved from https://hbr. org/2011/09/why-your-it-project-may-be-riskier-than-you-think

Gallup. (2017, February 7). *The cost of bad project management.* Retrieved from http://news.gallup.com/businessjournal/152429/cost-bad-project-management.aspx

PricewaterhouseCoopers. (2016). *21st global CEO survey*. Retrieved from https://www.pwc.com/gx/en/ceo-survey/2017/pwc-ceo-20th-survey-report-2017.pdf

Chapter 3

Tuckman, B. (1965). Developmental sequence in small groups. *Psychological Bulletin, 63*(6), 384-399.

Tuckman, B. (Spring 2001). Developmental sequence in small groups. *Group Facilitation: A Research and Applications Journal, 3*, 71-72.

Manges, K., Scott-Cawiezell, J., & Ward, M. (2016). Maximizing team performance: The critical role of the nurse leader. *Nursing Forum, 52*(1): 21-29.

Chapter 4

Society for Human Resource Management. (n.d.). *Placing dollar cost on turnover.* Retrieved from https://www.shrm.org/resourcesandtools/hr-topics/behavioral-competencies/critical-evaluation/pages/placing-dollar-costs-on-turnover.aspx

Chapter 5

Giesen, G., & Osborne, L. (n.d.). *Tuckman tweaked.* Retrieved from https://www.du.edu/human-resources/media/documents/tuckman-tweaked.pdf

Lencioni, P. (2002). *The five dysfunctions of a team: A leadership fable*. San Francisco, CA: Jossey-Bass.

Chapter 6

Sariel, S. (2007, June). *An integrated planning, scheduling and execution framework for multi-robot cooperation and coordination.* [Doctoral dissertation]. Retrieved from http://web.itu.edu.tr/sariel/thesis/sariel_PhD_Thesis_2007.pdf

Surbhi, S. (2016, November 4). Difference between coordination and cooperation. *Key Differences.* Retrieved from https://keydifferences.com/difference-between-coordination-and-cooperation.html#ixzz4tiH3IeCn

Dragisic, J. (2016). *The collaborative instinct.* North Charleston, SC: Create Space.

Markova, D., & McArthur, A. (2015). *Collaborative intelligence: Thinking with people who think differently.* New York, NY: Spiegel & Grau.

Osunmakinde, I. (2016). Multi-robot coordination. In J. Roul, & A. Gopal, *Mobile Intelligence.* Boca Raton, FL: CRC Press.

II: THE BRAIN SCIENCE OF GROUPS & TEAMS

Harris, Z. (2014). *The neuroscience of building teams.* Retrieved from https://www.youtube.com/watch?v=uxqqi1dd_UA

Chapter 7

Brown, B. (2013). *Daring greatly: How the courage to be vulnerable transforms the way we live, love, parent, and lead.* New York, NY: Penguin Publishing Group.

Chapter 8

Hasson, U., et al. (2012). Brain-to-brain coupling: a mechanism for creating and sharing a social world. *Trends in Cognitive Science, 16*(2), 93-136.

Silbert, L., et al. (2014). Coupled neural systems underlie the production and comprehension of naturalistic narrative speech. *Proceedings of the National Academy of Sciences, 111*(43), E4687-E4696.

Stephens, G., Silbert, L., & Hasson, U. (2010). Speaker–listener neural coupling underlies successful communication. *Proceedings of the National Academy of Sciences, 107*(32), 14425-14430.

Lieberman, M. (2017). The neuroscience of teams. Presentation at the NeuroLeadership Summit. Live-streamed at https://summit. neuroleadership.com

Chapter 9

Rizzolatti, G., Pavesi, G., & Fadiga, L. (1995, June 1). Motor facilitation during action observation: a magnetic stimulation study. *American Physiological Society, 73*(6), 2608-2611.

Iocaboni, M. (2009). *Mirroring people: The science on how we connect to others.* New York, NY: Pan Books Limited.

Hopwood, C. (2016, July 16). Don't do what I do: How getting out of sync can help relationships. In *Shots: Health News from NPR.* Retrieved from https://www.npr.org/sections/health-shots/2016/07/16/485721853/ dont-do-what-i-do-how-getting-out-of-sync-can-help-relationships

Khader, N. (2014, August 14). The Danish model for prevention of radicalization and extremism. *Hudson Institute.* Retrieved from https://www. hudson.org/research/10555-the-danish-model-for-prevention-of-radicalization-and-extremism

Rosin, H. (2016, July 15). How a Danish town helped young Muslims turn away from ISIS. *Shots: Health News from NPR.* Retrieved from https:// www.npr.org/sections/health-shots/2016/07/15/485900076/how-a-danish-town-helped-young-muslims-turn-away-from-isis

Cracco, E., De Coster, L., Andres, M., & Brass, M. (2015, December). Motor simulation beyond the dyad: Automatic imitation of multiple actors. *Journal of Experimental Psychology: Human Perception and Performance, 41*(6), 1488-1501.

Cracco, E., De Coster, L., Andres, M., & Brass, M. (2016). Mirroring multiple agents: motor resonance during action observation is modulated by the number of agents. *Social Cognitive and Affective Neuroscience, 11*(9), 1422-1427.

Winerman, L. (2005, October). The mind's mirror. *American Psychological Association*. Retrieved from https://www.apa.org/monitor/oct05/mirror.aspx

Chapter 10

Vrticka, P., Andersson, F., Sander, D., & Vuilleumier, P. (2009). Memory for friends or foes: The social context of past encounters with faces modulates their subsequent neural traces in the brain. *Social Neuroscience, 4*(5), 384-401.

Goclowka, M., et al. (2015). Cooperative, competitive, and individualist. *International Journal of Psychology, 52*(3), 180-188.

Stevens, R.H., Galloway, T.L., Wang, P., & Berka, C. (2012). Cognitive neurophysiologic synchronies: what can they contribute to the study of teamwork? *Human Factors, 54*(4), 489-502.

Dikker S., Silbert L.J., Hasson U., & Zevin, J.D. (2014). On the same wavelength: predictable language enhances speaker-listener brain-to-brain synchrony in posterior superior temporal gyrus. *The Journal of Neuroscience, 34*(18), 6267-6272.

Stevens, R.H., & Galloway, T.L. (2014). Modeling the neurodynamics organizations and interactions of teams. *Social Neuroscience, 11*(2), 123-139.

Chapter 11

Taylor, R.P., et al. (2017). Seeing shapes in seemingly random spatial patterns: Fractal analysis of Rorschach inkblots. *Plos One, 12*(2), 1-17.

Likens, A.D., Amazeen, P.G., Stevens, R., Galloway, T., & Gorman, J.C. (2014). Neural signatures of team coordination are revealed by multifractal analysis. *Social Neuroscience, 9*(3), 219-234.

Williams, F. (2017, January 26). Why fractals are so soothing. *The Atlantic*. Retrieved from https://www.theatlantic.com/science/archive/2017/01/why-fractals-are-so-soothing/514520

III: THE BRAIN SCIENCE OF SAFETY & BELONGING

Edmondson, A. (2012). *Teaming: How organizations learn, innovate, and compete in the knowledge economy*. San Francisco, CA: Jossey-Bass.

Chapter 12

MacLean, P.D. (1990). *The triune brain in evolution: Role in paleocerebral functions*. New York, NY: Plenum Press.

Lieberman, M. (2013). *Social: Why our brains are wired to connect*. New York, NY: Crown.

Kiverstein, J., & Miller, M. (2015). The embodied brain: towards a radical embodied cognitive neuroscience. *Frontiers in Human Neuroscience, 9*, 237.

Chapter 13

National Institute for Occupational Safety and Health (2006). *Workplace violence prevention and research needs.* Retrieved from: https://www.cdc.gov/niosh/topics/violence/fastfacts.html

Edmondson, A. (1999). Psychological safety and learning behavior in work teams. *Administrative Science Quarterly, 44*(2), 350-383.

Comaford, C. (2016, August 27). 75% of workers are affected by bullying: Here's what to do about it. *Forbes.* Retrieved from https://www.forbes.com/sites/christinecomaford/2016/08/27/the-enormous-toll-workplace-bullying-takes-on-your-bottom-line/#4ab2be205595

Workplace Bullying Institute. (n.d.). *Definition of workplace bullying.* Retrieved from http://www.workplacebullying.org/individuals/problem/definition

Workplace Violence Fact Sheet. (2016). *Office for victims of crime.* Retrieved from: https://ovc.ncjrs.gov/ncvrw2016/content/section-6/PDF/2016NCVRW_6_WorkplaceViolence-508.pdf

Edmondson, A., & Zhike, L. (2014). Psychological safety: The history, renaissance, and future of an interpersonal construct. *Annual Review of Organizational Psychology and Organizational Behavior, 1,* 23-43.

Duhigg, C. (2016, February 25). What Google learned from its quest to build the perfect team. *New York Times.* Retrieved from https://www.nytimes.com/2016/02/28/magazine/what-google-learned-from-its-quest-to-build-the-perfect-team.html

Edmondson, A. (2012). *Teaming: How organizations learn, innovate, and compete in the knowledge economy.* San Francisco, CA: Jossey-Bass.

Chapter 14

DeWall, N.C., et al. (2010). Acetaminophen reduces social pain: Behavioral and neural evidence. *Psychological Science, 21*(7), 931-937.

Weir, K. (2012, April). The pain of social rejection. *American Psychological Association.* Retrieved from https://www.apa.org/monitor/2012/04/rejection.aspx

Brown, B. (2013). *Daring greatly: How the courage to be vulnerable transforms the way we live, love, parent, and lead.* New York, N.Y: Penguin Publishing Group.

Cikara, M., & Van Bavel, J.J. (2014, May 6). The neuroscience of intergroup relations: An integrative review. *Association for Psychological Science, 9*(3), 245-274.

Thomas, C., et al. (2008). Reduced structural connectivity in ventral visual cortex in congenital prosopagnosia. *Nature Neuroscience, 12,* 29-31.

Tsao, D.Y., et al. (2006). A cortical region consisting entirely of face-selective cells. *Science, 311*(5761), 670-674. Retrieved from http://science.sciencemag.org/content/311/5761/670

Parvizi, J., et al. (October 2012). Electrical stimulation of human fusiform face-selective regions distort perception. *Journal of Neuroscience, 32*(43), 14915-14920.

Gobbini, M.I., & Haxby, J.V. (2007). Neural systems for recognition of familiar faces. *Neuropsychologia, 45*(1), 32-41.

Grens, K. (2014, November 1). A face to remember. *The Scientist*. Retrieved from https://www.the-scientist.com/?articles.view/articleNo/41326/title/A-Face-to-Remember

Vrticka, P., Andersson, F., Sander, D., & Vuilleumier, P. (2009). Memory for friends or foes: The social context of past encounters with faces modulates their subsequent neural traces in the brain. *Social Neuroscience, 4*(5), 384-401.

Cikara, M., & Van Bavel, J.J. (2014, May 6). The neuroscience of intergroup relations: An integrative review. *Association for Psychological Science, 9*(3), 245-274.

Smith, D.L. (2011). *Less than human: Why we demean, enslave, and exterminate others*. New York, N.Y: St. Martin's Press.

Brown, B. (2017). *Braving the wilderness: The quest for true belonging and the courage to stand alone*. New York, N.Y: Penguin Publishing Group.

Maiese, M. (2003, July). What it means to dehumanize. *Beyond Intractability*. Retrieved from https://www.beyondintractability.org/essay/dehumanization

Eichenwald, K. (2012, August). Microsoft's lost decade. *Vanity Fair*. Retrieved from https://www.vanityfair.com/news/business/2012/08/microsoft-lost-mojo-steve-ballmer

Chapter 15

Guassi, Moreira, J. F., Van Bavel, J. J., & Telzer, E. H. (2017). The neural development of "us and them." *Social Cognitive and Affective Neuroscience, 12*(2), 184-196.

Ratner, K.G., Kaul, C., & Van Bavel, J.J. (2013, October 1). Is race erased? Decoding race from patterns of neural activity when skin color is not diagnostic of group boundaries. *Social Cognitive and Affective Neuroscience, 8*(7), 750–755.

Gerbner, G., & Gross, L. (1976). Living with television: The violence profile. *Journal of Communication, 26*(2), 172-194.

Hundt, R. (1996, February 9). Speech: *Television, kids, indecency, violence, and the public interest*. Delivered at Duke Law Journal's 27th Annual Administrative Law Conference. Retrieved from https://transition.fcc.gov/Speeches/Hundt/spreh605.txt

Stossel, S. (1997, May). The man who counts the killings. *The Atlantic*. Retrieved from https://www.theatlantic.com/magazine/archive/1997/05/the-man-who-counts-the-killings/376850

Cook, G. (2013, Oct. 22). Why we are wired to connect. *Scientific American*. Retrieved from https://www.scientificamerican.com/article/why-we-are-wired-to-connect

Steele, C.M., & Aronson, J. (1995). Stereotype threat and the intellectual test performance of African Americans. *Journal of Personality and Social Psychology, 69*(5), 797-811.

England, C. (2016, October 25). Iceland's women leave work at 2:38 pm to protest gender pay gap. *Independent*. Retrieved from http://www.independent.co.uk/news/world/europe/iceland-women-protest-strike-gender-pay-gap-leave-work-early-a7378801.html

Zarya, V. (2017, June 7). The 2017 Fortune 500 includes a record number of women CEOs. *Fortune*. Retrieved from http://fortune.com/2017/06/07/fortune-women-ceos

LGBT Rights. (n.d.). In *Human Rights Watch*. Retrieved from https://www.hrw.org/topic/lgbt-rights

Gender, Sexuality, & Identity. (n.d.). In *Amnesty International*. Retrieved from https://www.amnestyusa.org/issues/gender-sexuality-identity

Aljazerra. (2017, July 17). *CAIR: Hate crimes against Muslims spike after Trump win*. Retrieved from https://www.aljazeera.com/news/2017/07/cair-hate-crimes-muslims-spike-trump-win-170718034249621.html

Good, C., Aronson, J., & Inzlicht, M. (2003). Improving adolescents' standardized test performance: An intervention to reduce the effects of stereotype threat. *Applied Developmental Psychology, 24*, 645-662.

Yong, E. (2013). Armor against prejudice. *Scientific American, 308*, 76-80.

IV: THE BRAIN SCIENCE OF INCLUSION & TRUST

Cox, C., et al. (2016). The science of inclusion: how we can leverage the brain to build smarter teams. *Neuroleadership Journal, 6*, 4-16.

Chapter 16

Tavares, R.M., et al. (2015). A map for social navigation in the human brain. *Neuron, 87*(1), 231-243.

DeWall, N.C., & Bushman, B.J. (2011). Social acceptance and rejection: The sweet and the bitter. *Current Directions in Psychological Science, 20*, 256-260.

Williams, K.D., & Nida., S.A. (2011). Ostracism: Consequences and coping. *Psychological Science, 20*(2), 71-75.

Eisenberger, N.I. (2012). The neural bases of social pain: Evidence for shared representations with physical pain. *Psychosomatic Medicine, 74*(2), 126-135.

Kross, E., Berman, M.G., Mischel, W., Smith, E.E., & Wager, T.D. (2011). Social rejection shares somatosensory representations with physical pain. *Proceedings of the National Academy of Sciences of the United States of America, 108*(15), 6270-6275.

Cox, C., et al. (2016). The science of inclusion: how we can leverage the brain to build smarter teams. *Neuroleadership Journal, 6,* 4-16.

Chapter 17

Williams, K.D., & Nida, S.A. (2011). Ostracism: Consequences and coping. *Current Directions in Psychological Science, 20*(2), 71.

Weir, K. (2012, April). The pain of social rejection. *American Psychological Association.* Retrieved from https://www.apa.org/monitor/2012/04/rejection.aspx

Pearson, C., & Porath, C. (2009). *The cost of bad behavior: How incivility is damaging your business and what to do about it.* New York: N.Y. Grand Central Publishing.

The Associated Press. (2017, November 16). Las Vegas shooter Stephen Paddock, family battled mental issues, legal troubles. *Fox News.* Retrieved from http://www.foxnews.com/us/2017/11/06/las-vegas-shooter-stephen-paddock-family-battled-mental-issues-legal-troubles.html

NBC News. (n.d.). Texas church shooting. *NBC.* Retrieved from https://www.nbcnews.com/storyline/texas-church-shooting

CNN (2018, February 18). Florida school shooting victims demand tougher gun laws. *CNN.* Retrieved from https://www.cnn.com/2018/02/17/us/florida-school-shooting/index.html

Is your workplace prone to violence? (n.d.) In National Safety Council. Retrieved from http://www.nsc.org/Measure/Pages/Workplace-Violence.aspx

Rosin, H. (2016, July 15). How a Danish town helped young Muslim turn away from ISIS. *NPR.* Retrieved from https://www.npr.org/sections/health-shots/2016/07/15/485900076/how-a-danish-town-helped-young-muslims-turn-away-from-isis

Whitehouse, K. (2017, November 1). NYC terror suspects allegedly asked to hang ISIS flag in hospital room. *New York Post.* Retrieved from https://nypost.com/2017/11/01/nyc-truck-attack-suspect-faces-terrorism-charges

Weir, K. (2012). The pain of social rejection. *American Psychological Association.* Retrieved from https://www.apa.org/monitor/2012/04/rejection.aspx

Chapter 18

Quigley, J. (2014). Do you care about onboarding? You should [Infographic]. *Bamboo HR.* Retrieved from https://www.bamboohr.com/blog/onboarding-infographic

Andreatta, B. (2011). *Navigating the research university: A guide for first-year students (3rd ed).* Independence, KY: Cengage.

Tinto, V. (1987). *Leaving college: Rethinking the causes and cures of student attrition.* Chicago, IL: Chicago University Press.

Sue, D.W. (2010). *Microaggressions in everyday life: Race, gender and sexual orientation.* San Francisco, CA: Wiley.

Sue, D.W., et al. (2007). Racial microaggressions in everyday life: Implications for clinical practice. *American Psychologist, 62*(4), 271-286.

Cox, C., et al. (2016). The science of inclusion: how we can leverage the brain to build smarter teams. *Neuroleadership Journal, 6,* 4-16.

Hein, G., Silani, G., Preuschoff, K., Batson, C.D., & Singer, T. (2010). Neural responses to ingroup and outgroup members' suffering predict individual differences in costly helping. *Neuron, 68*(1),149-160.

Novembre, G., Zanon, M., & Silani, G. (2015). Empathy for social exclusion involves the sensory-discriminative component of pain: a within-subject fMRI study. *Social Cognitive and Affective Neuroscience, 10*(2), 153-164.

Bergland, C. (2014, March 3). The Neuroscience of social pain. *Psychology Today.* Retrieved from https://www.psychologytoday.com/blog/the-athletes-way/201403/the-neuroscience-social-pain

Beckes, L., Coan J.A., & Hasselmo, K. (2013). Familiarity promotes the blurring of self and other in the neural representation of threat. *Social Cognitive and Affective Neuroscience, 8*(6) 670-677.

Goleman, D., & Davidson, R.J. (2017). *Altered traits: Science reveals how meditation changes your mind, brain, and body.* New York, N.Y: Penguin Random House.

Chapter 19

Myers, V. (2014, November). How to overcome our biases? Walk boldly towards them [Video File]. *TEDxBeaconStreet.* Retrieved from https://www.ted.com/talks/verna_myers_how_to_overcome_our_biases_walk_boldly_toward_them?language=en

Yoshino, K., & Smith, C. (2014, March). Fear of being different stifles talent. *Harvard Business Review.* Retrieved from https://hbr.org/2014/03/fear-of-being-different-stifles-talent

Yoshino, K., & Smith, C. (2013, December). Uncovering talent: A new model of inclusion. *Deloitte University.* Retrieved from https://www2.deloitte.com/content/dam/Deloitte/us/Documents/about-deloitte/us-inclusion-uncovering-talent-paper.pdf

Brown, B. (2017). *Braving the wilderness: The quest for true belonging and the courage to stand alone.* New York, NY: Penguin Publishing Group.

Chapter 20

PricewaterhouseCoopers. (2016). *20th Global CEO Survey.* Retrieved from https://www.pwc.com/gx/en/ceo-survey/2016/landing-page/pwc-19th-annual-global-ceo-survey.pdf

Great Place To Work. (n.d.). *The business case for a high-trust culture.* Retrieved from https://www.greatplacetowork.com/business-case

Zak, Paul. (2017). The neuroscience of trust. *Harvard Business Review.* Retrieved from https://hbr.org/2017/01/the-neuroscience-of-trust

Shamay-Tsoory, S.G., et al. (2013). Giving peace a chance: oxytocin increases empathy to pain in the context of the Israeli-Palestinian conflict. *International Society of Psychneuroendocrinology, 38*(12), 3139-3144.

Zak, P. (2017). *Trust factor: The science of creating high-performance companies.* New York, NY: AMACOM Books.

Kouzes, J.M., & Posner, B. (2012). *The leadership challenge.* San Francisco, CA: Jossey-Bass.

Feltman, C. (2009). *The thin book of trust: An essential primer for building trust at work.* Bend, OR: Think Book Publishing.

Brown, B. (2017). *Braving the wilderness: The quest for true belonging and the courage to stand alone.* New York, NY: Penguin Publishing Group.

Hurst, A. (2016). *The purpose economy.* Boise, ID: Elevate Publishing.

Hurst, A., & Tavis, A. (2015). *Workforce purpose index 2015.* Imperative. Retrieved from https://cdn.imperative.com/media/public/Purpose_Index_2015

Frankl, V.E. (2006). *Man's search for meaning.* Boston, MA: Beacon Press.

V: THE FOUR GATES TO TEAM PERFORMANCE™

Zak, P. (2017). *Trust factor: The science of creating high-performance companies.* New York, NY: AMACOM Books.

Chapter 21

Hurst, A., & Tavis, A. (2015). *Workforce purpose index 2015.* Imperative. Retrieved from https://cdn.imperative.com/media/public/Purpose_Index_2015

Chapter 22

Edmonson, A. (1999). Psychology safety and learning behavior in work teams. *Administrative Science Quarterly, 44*(2), 350-383.

Flade, P., Asplund, J., & Elliot, G. (2015, October 8). Employees who use their strengths outperform those who don't. *Gallup News.* Retrieved from http://news.gallup.com/businessjournal/186044/employees-strengths-outperform-don.aspx

Finkelstein, S. (2017, October 29). Why companies should hire teams, not individuals. *Wall Street Journal.*

VI: STRATEGIES FOR EXECUTIVES, TEAM LEADERS, & TEAM MEMBERS

Benincasa, R. (2012). *How winning works: 8 essential leadership lessons from the toughest teams on earth*. Toronto, Canada: Harlequin.

Chapter 24

Edmondson, A.C. (2003). Managing the risk of learning: Psychological safety in work teams. In *International Handbook of Organizational Teamwork and Cooperative Working*. Chichester, UK: John Wiley & Sons.

Berman, R., & Johnson, R. (2017). *Star wars: The last jedi*. United States: LucasFilms/Walt Disney Pictures.

Chapter 25

Collins, J. (2001). *Good to great: Why some companies make the leap and others don't*. New York, NY: Harper.

Bersin, J. (2017). Global human capital trends 2017. *Deloitte University Press*. Retrieved from https://www2.deloitte.com/insights/us/en/focus/human-capital-trends/2017/learning-in-the-digital-age.html

Chapter 26

Cox, C., et al. (2016). The science of inclusion: how we can leverage the brain to build smarter teams. *Neuroleadership Journal, 6*, 4-16.

Chapter 27

Gordon, S. (2017). *Unconscious bias* [Video file]. Carpinteria, CA: LinkedIn Learning.

Wadors, P. (2017). *Diversity, inclusion and belonging* [Video file]. Carpinteria, CA: LinkedIn Learning.

Turnbull, H. (2015, November). *Helen Turnbull: Inclusion, exclusion, illusion and collusion* [Video file]. Retrieved from https://ed.ted.com/on/8wRtfCM3

Adichie, C. N. (2009, July). *Chimamanda Adichie: The danger of a single story* [Video file]. Retrieved from https://www.ted.com/talks/chimamanda_adichie_the_danger_of_a_single_story

Hoeks, V. (2014, July). *Valerie Hoeks: Cultural difference in business* [Video file]. Retrieved from https://www.youtube.com/watch?v=VMwjscSCcf0

Jobrani, M. (2010, July). *Maz Jobrani: Did you hear the one about the Iranian-American?* [Video file]. Retrieved from https://www.ted.com/talks/maz_jobrani_make_jokes_not_bombs

Mobley, M.S. (2013, March). *Dr. Marilyn Mobley: The paradox of diversity* [Video file]. Retrieved from http://www.tedxcle.com/dr-marilyn-sanders-mobley

Johson, A.G. (2017). *Privilege, power and difference (3rd ed)*. New York, NY: McGraw-Hill.

Myers, V. (2012). *Moving diversity forward: How to move from well-meaning to well-doing.* Chicago, IL: American Bar Association.

Brown, J. (2017). *Inclusion: Diversity, the new workplace, and the will to change.* Lake Forest, CA: Purpose Driven Publishing.

Scott, S. (2004). *Fierce conversations: Achieving success at work and in life, one conversation at a time.* Berkeley, CA: Berkeley Press.

Patterson, K., Grenny, J., & McMillan, R. (2011). *Crucial conversations: Tools for talking when stakes are high (2nd ed).* New York, NY: McGraw-Hill.

Andreatta, B. (2013). *Having difficult conversations* [Video file]. Carpinteria, CA: LinkedIn Learning.

Rath, T. (2007). *StrengthsFinder 2.0.* New York, NY: Gallup Press.

Hurst, A. (2016). *The purpose economy.* Boise, ID: Elevate Publishing.

Robinson, K. (2014). *Finding your element: How to discover your talents and passions and transform your life.* New York, NY: Penguin.

McKeown, G. (2014). *Essentialism: The disciplined pursuit of less.* New York, NY: Virgin.

Moore, T. (2009). *A life at work: The joy of discovering what you were born to do.* New York, NY: Harmony Books.

Palmer, P. (1999). *Let your life speak: Listening for the voice of vocation.* San Francisco, CA: Jossey-Bass.

Myss, C. (2003). *Sacred contracts: Awakening your divine potential.* New York, NY: Harmony Books.

Chapter 28

Andreatta, B. (2017). *Wired to resist: The brain sicence of why change fails and a new model for driving success.* Santa Barbara, CA: 7th Mind Publishing.

Books by Dr. Britt Andreatta

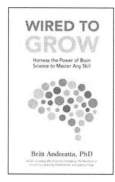

Available at Amazon, Barnes&Noble, iBooks, and Google.
Learn more at www.BrittAndreatta.com/books

ACKNOWLEDGMENTS: PRACTICING GRATITUDE

This book on teams is a product of my awesome team: Jenefer Angell (PassionfruitProjects.com) whose skill at editing makes writing books easy and rewarding, Leah Young (Leah-Young.com) who did the book layout in addition to editing my training videos and building my online learning platform (check out 7thMindInc.com), Claudia Arnett (BeTheMarket.com) handled all the story submissions and references in addition to managing my social media channels, and Shannan Troyer, who coordinates my speaking schedule and kept me organized when I took on way too many projects.

A special shout out to my fabulous colleagues who brought their expertise to reviewing the book: Linda Croyle (diversity and leadership; Croyle-Consulting.com), Kelly McGill (bias and inclusion; Linkedin.com/in/kellymcgill), and Lisa Slavid (innovation and leadership; LisaSlavid.com). A huge thank you to all the people who submitted case studies. This book is better for your sharing.

My gratitude also goes to the teams of neuroscientists and researchers who shared their work with me. Your insatiable curiosity and willingness to dig deeper benefit us all. A special thinks to the team at Deloitte and Ron Stevens for giving me permission to use their graphic images.

I'd also like to thank my home team: my wonderful husband Chris who keeps me going with hot tea and backrubs. My daughter Kiana who makes me laugh every day and who shares my love of colorful pens and highlighters. My soul kitties, Cody and Ellie, who sit on my keyboard every day, often adding unexpected edits to my manuscript. And to Pascal, the newest edition to our family. Who knew that chameleons were so cool? He spent many a day looking over my shoulder from his tree and reminding me that, yes, the reptilian brain is different very from the mammalian brain. And of course, my family and friends who put up with me through my hours of research and writing: Lisa, Pema, Dana, Elaine, Mike, Barbara, Roger, Kendra, and Carole.

Finally, to my tribe of leadership and learning professionals who work hard to bring out the best in their people and organizations. I am honored to share this important work with you.

I love teaming with you!

ABOUT THE AUTHOR

Dr. Britt Andreatta is an internationally recognized thought leader who creates science-based solutions for common workplace challenges. Drawing on her unique background in leadership, neuroscience, psychology and education, she has a profound understanding of how to unlock the best in people, helping organizations rise to their potential.

She is the CEO and President of 7th Mind, Inc., providing groundbreaking research and learning solutions that drive real behavior change. Britt has published several titles on learning and leadership including her books *Wired to Grow: Harness the Power of Brain Science to Master Any Skill* and *Wired to Resist: The Brain Science of Why Change Fails and a New Model for Driving Success*. Britt is currently writing her next books on the neuroscience of potential and the conscious evolution of organizations.

Britt is a seasoned professional with more than 25 years of experience consulting with businesses, universities, and nonprofit organizations. Corporate clients include Fortune 100 companies like Comcast, Microsoft, and Apple as well as companies such as Ernst & Young, Avvo, LinkedIn, Franklin Covey, AlterEco Foods, DPR Construction, Rustoleum, and Practice. Dr. Andreatta has also worked with major educational institutions like the University of California, Dartmouth University, and the University of New Mexico as well as nonprofit organizations like the YMCA and Norton Healthcare.

She has received over 8 million views worldwide of her courses on Lynda.com/LinkedIn Learning. Titles include *The Neuroscience of Learning, Leading with Emotional Intelligence, Creating a Culture of Learning, Having Difficult Conversations, Organizational Learning & Development*, and *Leading Change*. A highly sought-after and engaging speaker, Britt delivered a TEDx talk called "How Your Past Hijacks Your Future" and she regularly speaks at corporate events and international conferences receiving rave reviews like "best speaker of the conference" or "best keynote I've ever heard."

Britt has won several prestigious awards including the 2016 Global Training & Development Leadership Award from the World Training & Development Congress. She won the Gold Medal for *Chief Learning Officer* magazine's Trailblazer Award, and was also nominated for the CLO Strategy Award for her work in designing a performance management program based on growth mindset principles. *Talent Development* magazine identified her as an "outstanding thought leader and pioneer" and featured her in the June 2017 issue.

She has served as the Chief Learning Officer for Lynda.com and Senior Learning Consultant for global leadership and talent development at LinkedIn. She continues to partner with Lynda.com/LinkedIn as an author and thought leader on the brain science of success.

Dr. Andreatta has served as professor and dean at the University of California, Antioch University, and several graduate schools. She regularly consults with executives and organizations on how to maximize their full potential. To learn more, visit her website and social channels:

Website: www.BrittAndreatta.com

LinkedIn: www.linkedin.com/in/brittandreatta

Twitter: @BrittAndreatta

Take These Ideas Beyond the Page

If you are interested in bringing the Four Gates to Peak Team Performance™ to your organization, Dr. Britt Andreatta has created a range of science-based learning materials to help you. Her engaging keynotes, presentations, and workshops challenge assumptions and move audiences to action. Learn more by visiting www.BrittAndreatta.com/Wired-to-Connect or www.7thMindInc.com.